THE LIFE INSURANCE COUNSELOR

Federal Income Taxation of Life Insurance

American Bar Association
Real Property, Probate and Trust Law Section

Printed in the United States of America
Section of Real Property, Probate, and Trust Law
750 N. Lake Shore Drive, Chicago, IL 60611
94 93 92 91 90 5 4 3 2 1

Library of Congress Catalog Card Number 89-45609

The material contained herein represents the opinion of the authors and editors and should not be construed to be the action of either the American Bar Association or the Section of Real Property, Probate, and Trust Law unless adopted pursuant to the Bylaws of the Association.

Discounts are available for books ordered in bulk. Special consideration is given to state bars, CLE programs, and other bar-related organizations. Inquire at Publications Planning & Marketing, American Bar Association, 750 N. Lake Shore Drive, Chicago, IL 60611.

ISBN: 0-89707-463-7

Contents

Preface

The *Life Insurance Counselor* series of books is the result of many years of planning by members of several committees of the Real Property, Probate, and Trust Law Section of the American Bar Association, with encouragement and guidance from several sets of Supervisory Counsel Members and Committee Chairs.

As originally conceived, the *Counselor* was to be a life insurance primer for attorneys and other estate planning professionals to use in understanding life insurance illustrations—a so-called "how to" guide to analyzing life insurance illustrations and projections for the non-insurance specialist. The *Counselor* has, however, evolved into more than that.

The first book in the *Counselor* series, *Life Insurance Products, Illustrations, and Due Diligence*, is such a guide; but it also includes an extensive glossary of life insurance related terms and a discussion of the "due diligence" required of the estate planning professional in analyzing life insurance projections. This book utilizes as its basic format a series of illustrations for generic life insurance contracts of different types that have been "blown up" for ease of reference. They have also been extensively annotated to call the estate planner's attention to the most important items within the illustration.

The second book in the *Counselor* series, *Federal Income Taxation of Life Insurance*, is an exhaustive analysis of the federal income tax issues involved in the use of life insurance in estate planning. This book contains thirteen sections, dealing with each of the potential income tax issues raised by the use of life insurance in estate planning and presenting a detailed analysis of each.

The topics covered range from the I.R.C. definition of life insurance contracts, to an analysis of the Modified Endowment Contract provisions of TAMRA 88, to an analysis of the income tax issues relating to life insurance owned by the insured, to those issues relating to insurance provided by the insured's employer.

A third book in the *Counselor* series is planned. It will deal with the federal transfer tax issues relating to the use of life insurance in estate planning and will cover the federal gift, estate, and generation-skipping transfer tax aspects of using life insurance in estate planning (including the use of irrevocable life insurance trusts). The anticipated publication date of this book is late 1989.

Life Insurance Products, Illustrations, and Due Diligence is essentially the work product of the I-6 Task Force, under the direction of Michael D. Weinberg and David D. Addison, Co-Chairs. It draws upon the expertise of its authors, Richard A. Schwartz, FSA, and Catherine R. Turner, FSA, of M Financial Group of Portland, Oregon. This book could not have been produced without Dick and Cathy's help and dedication. We owe both of them and M Financial a debt of gratitude for sharing their time and knowledge. It was edited by Michael D. Weinberg.

Federal Income Taxation of Life Insurance was produced by the I-6 Task Force under the authorship of Donald O. Jansen, its Vice-Chair. Laila M. Asmar and Corinne B. Kahn, members of the I-6 Task Force, also contributed to the text. It was edited by Lawrence Brody.

The third book in the *Counselor* series will be a joint product of the C-6 and H-3 Committees, under the chairmanship of Lawrence Brody and Albert S. Barr, III, respectively.

The editors wish to express their thanks to everyone who participated in these projects, from conceptualization to working on the final products.

LAWRENCE BRODY
MICHAEL D. WEINBERG

Contributors

Donald O. Jansen

Donald O. Jansen is a partner in the law firm of Fulbright & Jaworski.

Mr. Jansen's professional activities include:

Federal Bar Association—past president, Houston chapter; past national deputy chairman, Younger Lawyers' Committee; past member of National Council; member of Federal Estate and Gift Taxation and Federal Election Law Committee.

American Bar Association—member of the Section of Real Property, Probate and Trust Law; member and past chairman of the Committee of Significant Current Literature, Probate and Trust Division; member of the Task Force on Legal Financial Planning, Probate and Trust Division.

State Bar of Texas—specialist in Estate Planning and Probate Law certified by the Texas Board of Legal Specialization; member of Real Estate, Probate and Trust Law Section; past Probate Editor of the Newsletter of Real Estate, Probate and Trust Law Section.

Louisiana State Bar Association

Houston Bar Association—former director of Probate, Trusts and Estates Section; member, American College of Probate Counsel.

Former legal counsel for the Houston Jaycees, the Texas Young Republican Federation, the 1980 Texas George Bush for President Campaign, and the Harris County Republican Party.

Captain, the Judge Advocate General Corps, U.S. Army (1963–66).

Speaker at numerous bar association and estate planning councils; and a contributing author.

Mr. Jansen received his B.B.A. and J.D. from Loyola University in New Orleans, and his LL.M. from Georgetown University in Washington, D.C.

Laila M. Asmar

Laila M. Asmar is an associate with the diversified financial services firm of Linscomb & Williams based in Houston, Texas. Linscomb & Williams is distinct in that it was established in 1971 and is one of the largest independent professionally staffed financial services firms in Texas.

Ms. Asmar received an accounting degree from the University of Southern Mississippi (B.S. in Bus. Adm.), a law degree from South Texas College of Law (J.D.), and has obtained the Certified Public Accountant designation (CPA) and the Certified Financial Planner designation (CFP). Prior to her current professional position, Ms. Asmar was employed by a Big Eight accounting firm and gained experience in both its audit and tax departments. Ms. Asmar furthered her tax experience in the corporate tax planning department of a Houston-based Fortune 500 company. Upon graduation from law school, Ms. Asmar was in private legal practice as an estate planning attorney with a prominent Austin law firm.

Ms. Asmar maintains memberships in the American Bar Association (member of Real Property, Probate and Trust Law Section), Texas Bar Association (member of Real Estate, Probate and Trust Law Section), Houston Young Lawyers Association, Association of Women Attorneys, the Texas Society of Certified Public Accountants, and the International Association of Financial Planners.

Ms. Asmar is a published casenote author and a contributing editor to a national employee benefit publication. Ms. Asmar has spoken before numerous professional groups regarding independent financial planning and services including seminars presented before the top executives of Fortune 500 companies. Ms. Asmar is active in community affairs by contributing her financial support and time to various charitable organizations serving the Houston area.

Corinne B. Kahn

Corinne B. Kahn was admitted to the bar 1978, New Jersey; 1988, Florida, United States District Court, District of New Jersey, 1978; United States Tax Court, 1980. Education: New York University (B.A. 1974); Hofstra University (J.D. 1977); Rutgers University (M.B.A. 1978). Published: "Irrevocable Lifetime Insurance Trust" CCH Estate and Financial Planning Reporter, 1984–1987. Member: The Florida Bar (member, Bankruptcy and Real Property, Probate and Trust Law Sections); Palm Beach County Bar Association; South Palm Beach County Bar Association; American Bar Association (member Section of Taxation, Real Property, Probate and Trust Law (Task Force on Legal Financial Planning) and Young Lawyers Sections); Director, Estate Planning Council of Broward County; Secretary, International Association for Financial Planning (Distinguished Service Award 1987–1988).

Lawrence Brody

Lawrence Brody is a partner in the St. Louis-based law firm of Bryan, Cave, McPheeters & McRoberts, a national and international law firm, where he is a member of the Tax and the Estates and Trusts Departments. Mr. Brody is a member of the Missouri, St. Louis, and American Bar Associations, a member of the American Bar Association Section of Taxation, and chairman of the Committee of Life Insurance of the American Bar Association Section of Real Property, Probate and Trust Law.

He is an adjunct professor in the graduate tax program at Washington University School of Law in St. Louis, Missouri, a fellow of the American College of Probate Counsel, a member of the Board of Contributing Editors of the American Society of CLUs and ChFCs *Keeping Current* series, and a member of the Editorial Board of *The Practical Accountant*.

Mr. Brody is a frequent speaker on estate planning on life insurance topics at local and national tax institutes and seminars and is the author or co-author of numerous articles on estate planning and life insurance issues. He co-authored the B.N.A. Tax Management Portfolio, "Insurance Related Compensation" and "Missouri Estate Planning Will Drafting and Estate Administration—Forms and Practice," Aspen Publishing Co. (1987).

FEDERAL INCOME TAXATION OF LIFE INSURANCE

For many years, life insurance has been the "fair-haired child" of the Internal Revenue Code receiving many tax benefits particularly in the income tax arena. For a policy with cash reserves, the income build up of the reserve remains income tax free, unless the policy is totally or partially surrendered. If the insured should die prior to the surrender of the policy, the proceeds (including the income build up of the cash value) is received income tax free except where there has been a transfer for value. Through third party ownership of the policy denying the insured incidents of ownership, the proceeds may be excluded from the insured's gross estate for federal estate tax purposes at a taxable gift cost to the insured (if he is the transferor) equal only to the value of the cash reserve and premium payments, most of which might be sheltered from gift taxation by the gift tax annual exclusion. In addition, generation-skipping taxes on insurance proceeds payable to a skip person can be avoided if the premium gifts are protected by the gift tax annual exclusion or the use of the generation-skipping tax exemption, although the former is not available for policies held in the typical life insurance trust.

This portion of the primer will discuss the general income tax rules in relation to receipt of insurance proceeds, the cash value growth within the life insurance policy, the deductibility of premium payments by an employer with the concommitant question of income taxation to the employee for premiums paid and an analysis of the deductibility of interest on loans against the cash surrender value of a policy. There will be an analysis of the rules for a tax free exchange of an insurance policy in these days when many older policies are being replaced. The income tax consequences of placing insurance in a trust or a qualified benefit plan as well as the use of insurance to fund deferred compensation agreements will be reviewed from the income tax viewpoint.

However, before we can review the special income tax rules applicable to a life insurance contract, it is first necessary to determine what insurance policies qualify as a "life insurance contract" under the Internal Revenue Code.

1. <u>Definition of "Life Insurance Contract"</u>

   The definition which applies to a particular life insurance policy will depend upon the issuance date of the policy. All insurance policies issued after 1984 must meet the definition supplied in IRC Section 7702.

Flexible premium policies (e.g., universal and adjustable life) issued before 1985 must meet the requirements of IRC Section 101(f). All single premium and periodic premium policies issued before 1985 are not subject to any express statutory definition but must conform with judicially developed precedent. Finally, variable life insurance policies, in addition to meeting whichever of the above definition of life insurance contract is applicable, must meet certain diversification requirements for insurance company taxable years beginning after 1983 under IRC Section 817(h) in order to prevent disqualification as a life insurance contract.

a. Pre-DEFRA rules for single or periodic premium contracts. As noted above, the Internal Revenue Code does not contain a definition of life insurance contract which is applicable to these policies. However, as early as 1941, the United States Supreme Court held that life insurance must involve risk-shifting and risk-distribution with the result that the issuance of a single premium life insurance policy at the time a single premium annuity contract is purchased negates risk-shifting. *Helvering v. LeGierse*, 312 U.S. 531, 539 (1941). The cash value portion of these policies is also included within the judicially recognized definition of life insurance contract as long as the cash reserve cannot be purchased separately from the pure insurance, the policyholder has no vested rights in the reserve, and the reserve cannot be received by the policyholder other than through total or partial surrender or loans. *Moseley v. Commissioner*, 72 T.C. 183 (1979), acq. 1980-1 C.B. 1. Thus, for non-flexible premium policies issued before 1985, there must be significant pure insurance coverage over and above the cash reserve for a policy to be treated as a life insurance contract. This will depend upon the facts of each case. Because of the uncertainty created by this fact question particularly with the advent of interest-sensitive policies in recent years, Congress passed legislation which established a "bright line" test for the definition of life insurance contract as applied to all flexible premium policies and to other whole life policies issued after 1985.

b. Pre-DEFRA rules for flexible premium policies. Because of questions arising as to whether certain universal and adjustable life policies met the judicial definition of life insurance contract for purposes of the Internal Revenue Code, Congress passed temporary legislation in the Tax Equity and Fiscal Responsibility Act ("TEFRA") which approved all flexible premium life insurance contracts but only if one of two tests was met to guarantee that there was a reasonable relationship between pure insurance coverage and policy cash values, with policies in existence on the date of TEFRA having a 12-month grace period in which to amend their contracts to comply with the new rules. The two alternative tests imposed by TEFRA are quite similar to the two tests eventually imposed by IRC Section 7702 on all life insurance contracts although they are somewhat more liberal with the possible result that more cash value can be accumulated under a universal life policy purchased before 1985 than under a universal life policy purchased after 1984.

According to the DEFRA Senate Finance Report, the grandfathering of flexible premium contracts issued before 1985 is lost if such a contract is exchanged (tax-free under IRC Section 1035 or otherwise) after 1984 with the result that the new contract must meet the new rules of Section 7702. The Senate Committee Report also states that a pre-1985 flexible premium contract will lose its grandfathering status if there is a post-1984 change in the contract affecting the amount or pattern of death benefit, the premium pattern, the rate or rates guaranteed on issuance of the contract, or mortality and expense charges but will not lose its grandfathered status if there is a change in minor administrative provisions or in a loan rate.

c. <u>Section 7702 definition of life insurance contract</u>. As indicated earlier, the permanent statutory definition of "life insurance contract" contained in IRC Section 7702 applies to all insurance contracts issued after 1984. If the applicable state law treats a life insurance contract as a single, integrated life insurance contract, the Code will treat it as a single contract of life insurance for federal tax purposes. However, if state law treats a policy as a combination of term life insurance with an annuity contract or a premium deposit fund, so will the federal law.

In order to ensure adequate risk-shifting and risk-distribution, Section 7702 requires that an insurance policy meet one of two tests in order to be a "life insurance contract" for federal tax purposes

-- (a) cash value accumulation test and (b) guideline premium and cash value corridor test. Briefly, the cash value accumulation test requires that, by terms of the contract, the cash surrender value may not at any time exceed the net single premium which would have to be paid at such time to fund future benefits assuming a maturity date of no earlier than age 95 of the insured or later than age 100. The cash value is determined without regard to surrender charges, policy loans or reasonable termination dividends. The net single premium is determined with an assumed interest rate of not greater than 4% or the rate guaranteed at the issuance of the contract, a mortality charge as specified in the policy (or, if none is specified, the mortality charge used in determining the contract statutory reserves). In order to prevent continuation of abuses by certain insurance carriers, the Technical and Miscellaneous Revenue Act ("TAMRA") of 1988 in calculating the net single premium would require the mortality charges in contracts entered into on or after October 21, 1988 to be reasonable and not in excess of the charges specified in the prevailing Commissioners' standard tables (except as provided in regulations for substandard or unknown risks). Until regulations are issued, mortality charges are reasonable if they do not materially differ from charges actually expected to be imposed by the carrier. The cash value accumulation test will generally be used to qualify the traditional whole life policy.

The guideline premium and cash value corridor test consists of two elements, both of which must be met. The guideline premium limitation (which prevents excessive premium payments compared to traditional policies) requires that the sum of premium payments cannot exceed at any time the greater of the guideline single premium at issue necessary to fund the future death benefits or the sum of guideline level premiums to date based upon a level annual amount necessary to fund future benefits until at least age 95. Both the guideline single premium and the guideline level premium are based upon the mortality charges specified in the contract (or, if none are specified, those used in determining the contract statutory reserves) and other charges specified in the contract. Note again that TAMRA would put certain reasonability limitations upon the mortality charges used in this formula for policies issued on or after October 21, 1988. In addition,

TAMRA requires that other expense charges specified in such policies be reasonably based upon the carrier's experience or, if none, upon industry-wide experience. The interest assumption in calculating the guideline single premium is the greater of 6% or the rate guaranteed at the issuance of the contract but, in regard to guideline level premiums, the rate is the greater of 4% or the rate guaranteed at the issuance of the contract.

The cash value corridor limitation (which prevents excessive build up of premium plus income relative to insurance risks) requires that the death benefit at any time be not less than the applicable percentage of cash surrender value (not reduced by surrender charges, policy loans and reasonable termination dividends). The following are the "applicable percentages":

In the case of an insured with an attained age as of the beginning of the contract year of:		The applicable percentage shall decrease by a ratable portion for each full year:	
More than:	But not more than	From:	To:
0	40	250	250
40	45	250	215
45	50	215	185
50	55	185	150
55	60	150	130
60	65	130	120
65	70	120	115
70	75	115	105
75	90	105	105
90	95	105	100

This second test (guideline premium and cash value corridor) is the test which will be generally used to qualify universal life and adjustable life policies.

In using these two tests, future benefits means death benefits and endowment benefits. However, certain "qualified additional benefits" will not themselves be treated as future benefits under the contract but charges for such qualified additional benefits will be treated as future benefits. The term "qualified additional benefits" means guaranteed insurability, accidental death or disability benefit, family term coverage, disability waiver of benefit, or other benefits prescribed under regulations. In determining premiums paid in applying these tests, the payment will be reduced by any dividends and any premium paid (including interest thereon) in excess of the limitations of Section 7702 if returned within 60 days after the end of the contract year but the interest portion of the refund will be subject to income taxation.

d. Special additional rule for variable life insurance contracts. A variable life insurance contract must clear one additional hurdle in meeting the definition of life insurance contract. IRC Section 817(h) requires that every variable life insurance contract (other than a pension plan contract which is based on one or more segregated asset accounts) must either meet the safe harbor diversification requirements of the statute or the diversification requirements of Treasury regulations. Reg. Sec. 1.817-5T. Except for a start up period of one year (five years for a segregated real property account), the diversification test must be met on the last day or within thirty days of the last day of each calendar year quarter. Furthermore, in applying the definition of life insurance contract under Section 7702, the variable life insurance contract must meet such definition whenever the death benefits under the contract change but not less frequently than once during each 12-month period.

2. Proceeds Payable at Death of Insured.

a. General Rule. With the exceptions noted below, generally, gross income of a beneficiary of a life insurance contract does not include the amounts received from such contract paid by reason of the death of the insured. IRC Section 101(a)(1). The exclusion applies whether the payment is to the estate of the insured or to any beneficiary (individual, corporation or partnership) and whether it is made directly or in trust. The exclusion also applies whether the payment is in a single sum or in installments (although the interest element of the installments will be subject to income taxation). The death benefit includes benefits payable at death under workman's compensation insurance contracts, endowment contracts or accident and health insurance contracts. Reg. Sec. 1.101-1(a)(1). The exclusion extends to proceeds from indexed additions to the original insurance in the form of paid-up additions or term insurance riders. P.L.R. 8111054. The exclusion includes the portion of the proceeds represented by the cash surrender value immediately before death including any accumulated income in that cash value.

The proceeds must be paid because of the death of the insured. If they are paid during the lifetime of the insured, Section 101(a)(1) does not apply and the rules of taxation concerning any cash value growth of the policy are determined under IRC Section 72. An explanation of these rules is contained in item 3. Whether proceeds are payable by reason of the death of the insured is based upon the good faith determination of the insurance company based on the facts and circumstances indicating death or on a presumption of death under applicable state law as was the case involving payments of proceeds on the life of a missing in action member of the armed forces when there was no official finding of death by the Department of Defense. Rev. Rul. 78-372, 1978-2 C.B. 93.

b. Exception if Policy Does Not Meet Definition of Life Insurance Contract. An insurance policy is covered under the provisions of Section 101(a)(1) only if it is a "life insurance contract." As noted earlier, the applicable definition of life insurance contract will depend upon the issuance date of the policy. Policies issued after 1984 are subject to a definition of life insurance contract contained in IRC Section 7702. *See* item 1 for a discussion of the definition of life insurance contract both before and after the passage of Section 7702. In addition to meeting the federal definition of life insurance contract, the policy must also be considered a life insurance contract under applicable state or foreign law. IRC Section 7702(a). For example, local law usually does not treat a policy as life insurance unless the owner of the policy has an insurable interest in the life of the insured. *Ducros v. Commissioner*, 272 F.2d 49 (6th Cir. 1959).

If the entire policy is not considered a life insurance contract under applicable state or foreign law, the entire proceeds payable at the death of the insured, less any investment in the contract by the policy owner, will be included in the gross income of the beneficiary. Presumably, if only part of the policy is not considered to be life insurance under applicable state or foreign law such as where state law treats a policy as a combination of term life insurance and an annuity contract, the proceeds from the portion of the policy considered life insurance under local law should still be excludable from the beneficiary's income if the additional requirements of federal law are met.

If a policy issued after 1984 which is a life insurance contract under applicable state or foreign law fails to meet the definition of life insurance contract contained in Section 7702 of the Code, then there is not a total disallowance of the exclusion under Section 101(a)(1) but there is a partial exclusion of the death proceeds equal to the amount by which they exceed the net surrender value (the cash surrender value with regard to surrender charges but without regard to policy loans) immediately prior to death of the insured. IRC Section 7702(g)(2). The tax consequences on the income accumulation in the cash surrender value of a life insurance contract which fails to meet one of the two tests contained in Section 7702 is discussed in item 3.

As noted earlier, flexible premium policies issued before 1985 are subject to a special life insurance contract definition which is in many ways similar to the provisions of Section 7702. IRC Section 101(f). However, unlike Section 7702(g), Section 101(f) does not expressly give a partial exemption of the death proceeds in excess of the cash surrender value should the policy fail to meet one of the two alternative tests contained in that Section. Without any authorities on the issue, there are two ways of treating the tax consequences of a disqualified flexible premium policy issued before 1985. One way is to include in the beneficiary's gross income the entire death proceeds to the extent they exceed the investment in the contract. The other approach is to treat the proceeds as being paid from a bifurcated policy consisting of term insurance and a cash side fund with the term insurance portion of the premiums being excludible under Section 101(a)(1).

With regard to single or periodic premium policies issued before 1985 which fail to meet the judicially imposed risk-shifting and risk-distribution tests for the definition of life insurance contract, the entire proceeds payable at death less any investment in the contract will be includable in the gross income of the beneficiary. *Barnes v. United States*, 801 F.2d 984 (7th Cir. 1986).

c. <u>Exception If Proceeds Paid At Date Later Than Death</u>. If the insurance company pursuant to a settlement option or otherwise delays the payment of all or part of the proceeds of an insurance policy at the death of the insured, any interest attributable to such delay in payment will be includable in the gross income of the beneficiary.

If the proceeds are held under an agreement to pay interest thereon, the total interest payment will be included in gross income. IRC Section 101(c). This statute applies whether the election to have an amount held under an agreement to pay interest is made by the insured, by his beneficiaries or by his estate and whether or not an interest rate is expressly stated in the agreement. This provision applies only to payments made by the insurer. The total inclusion of payments as interest does not apply to installment payments of death proceeds which will normally result in only a part of the payment being interest which will be discussed below. However, in order for the installment payment rules to apply, the payment from the insurance carrier must represent a substantial diminution of the principal amount of the death proceeds. Reg. Sec. 1.101-3(a).

If the death proceeds are held by the insurer under an agreement provided for in the life insurance contract, whether as an option or otherwise, to pay the amount in installments after the death of the insured, the present value of those proceeds at the insured's death will be prorated over the time of installment payments with any excess payments being includable in the beneficiary's income as interest. IRC Section 101(d). The present value of the payments for proration purposes is to be determined by using the interest rate used by the insurer in calculating the payments under the agreement and, the mortality table specified in the insurance contract for insureds dying before October 23, 1986 or the unisex mortality table specified in Reg. Sec. 1.101-7T for insureds dying after October 22, 1986. The regulations go into considerable detail in determining proration when payments are made to a sole beneficiary, two or more beneficiaries, or secondary beneficiaries and when payments are not made periodically or are received under a family income rider. Reg. Sec. 1.101-4(c), (d), (f) and (h). There is no interest inclusion under the installment option if the amounts payable under the option cannot exceed the amount payable at the time of the insured's death. Reg. Sec. 1.101-4(a)(1)(i). Furthermore, in the case of an insurance policy which was the subject of a transfer for value, the exclusion of principal by proration cannot exceed the consideration paid by the transferee plus other premiums and considerations paid subsequent to the transfer. Reg. Sec. 1.101-4(b)(3).

In connection with insureds who died before October 23, 1986, a surviving spouse is able to exclude from income up to $1,000 a year of interest on installment payments of life insurance proceeds. Former Section 101(d)(1)(B). Tax Reform Act of 1986 ("TRA 86") Section 421(b)(2). A surviving spouse means the spouse of the insured as of the date of death, including a spouse legally separated but not under a decree of absolute divorce. Reg. Sec. 1.101-3(a)(ii). There is only a $1,000 exclusion even though there are several insurance policies on the life of the same insured subject to the installment option in favor of the spouse. Reg. Sec. 1.101-4(a)(2). Presumably, since the exclusion is tied to the surviving spouse of "the insured" a spouse who is receiving installments for proceeds of insurance payable upon the death of two different insured-spouses would receive a separate exclusion of up to $1,000 a year of interest on installment payments on proceeds from the policies on the life of each deceased insured-spouse. The $1,000 interest exclusion is still available to a spouse after remarriage. Rev. Rul. 72-164, 1972-1 C.B. 28. The $1,000 exclusion is not available for interest received by a spouse under an interest only option. However, should the surviving spouse change the option from interest only to an installment payment option, the $1,000 a year exclusion will apply to the interest on the installment payments. Rev. Rul. 65-284, 1965-2 C.B. 28.

d. <u>Exception for Transfer for Valuable Consideration</u>. After the initial issuance of a policy if it is subsequently transferred for consideration, then the income exclusion under Section 101(a)(1) is lost and the beneficiary will have to include in his gross income proceeds received at the death of the insured to the extent that they exceed the consideration paid and the premiums and other amounts subsequently paid by the transferee. IRC Section 101(a)(2). If there is a gratuitous transfer of the policy, the proceeds still qualify for exclusion from income if they were excludable prior to the transfer. Reg. Sec. 1.101-1(b)(2). As noted in more detail below, there are exceptions to the transfer for value rule if the transfer is to the insured, his partner, his partnership, or a corporation in which he is a shareholder of officer or if the transferee's basis is determined in whole or in part by reference to the basis of the transferor. IRC Section 101(a)(2)(A) and (B).

(1) <u>What is a Transfer for Value</u>? It is an absolute transfer for value of a right to receive all or a part of the proceeds of a life insurance policy. However, the pledging or assignment of a policy as a collateral security is not a transfer for value. Reg. Sec. 1.101-1(b)(4). Since the statute covers the transfer of a life insurance contract or any interest therein, the transfer for value rule can be triggered without the transfer of the ownership of the policy such as by the creation of an enforceable contractual right to receive all or any part of the proceeds of the policy. Thus, a transfer of an insurance policy to a non-insured shareholder by a corporation in liquidation was a transfer for value. *Charles E. Lambeth*, 38 B.T.A. 351 (1938). When insurance policies were assigned by a corporation and one shareholder to two non-insured shareholders as part of a stock purchase arrangement, there was a transfer for value and the portion of the premiums paid on the policy after the transfer by shareholders who were not the owners of the policy did not count as consideration paid by the owners after the transfer. *Monroe v. Patterson*, 197 F.Supp. 146 (N.D. Ala. 1961). If a corporation sells an insurance policy to the wife of the insured, the transaction is a transfer for value. *Estate of Rath v. United States*, 608 F.2d 254 (6th Cir. 1979). However, an option to purchase an insurance policy even if purchased for valuable consideration does not trigger the transfer for value rule since it is a personal right and not an enforceable right against the insurance contract although the exercise of the option could be a transfer for value. *Estate of Rath v. United States, supra.*

(2) Exceptions to Transfer for Value Rule. The Code lists five exceptions to the transfer for value rule even though the transfer is for valuable consideration.

(a) Commonality of Basis. If the transferee's basis in the policy is determined in whole or in part by reference to the basis of the policy in the hands of the transferor, the transfer is exempt from the transfer for value rule. IRC Section 101(a)(2)(A). Thus if the policy was transferred partially as a gift and partially for value, the entire policy is exempt from the transfer for value rule since the basis for the gift portion remains the same in the hands of the transferee. For example, if a policy subject to a loan is transferred by gift, there is a transfer for value to the extent of the policy loan but, when the transferor's basis exceeded the amount of the loan, the transferee's basis was partially determined by the transferor's basis and the transfer fell within this exception. Rev. Rul. 69-187, 1969-1 C.B. 45. P.L.R. 8027113. P.L.R. 8628007. Presumably, if the amount of the loan exceeded the transferor's basis in the policy, the transfer for value rule would apply since the transferee's basis would be equal to the amount of the loan and would not be determined in part by the transferor's basis.

After July 18, 1984, transfers of property for consideration between former spouses (but only if the transfer is incident to the divorce) or between spouses without regard to divorce are treated as gifts and the transferee has the transferor's basis. IRC Section 1041. Thus, if insurance policies are transferred pursuant to a property settlement in a divorce the exception to the transfer for value rule would apply since the transferee spouse's basis is the same as that of the transferor.

Outside of the divorce situation, this new statute is useful in instances where the insured wishes to transfer an insurance policy to an irrevocable life insurance trust or to children and avoid the three year estate tax inclusion rule of IRC Section 2035. The insured could sell the policy to his or her spouse for full value (the spouse using his or her separate funds) and then the spouse could transfer the policy to the children or the trust. Since the spouse has the same basis as the insured in the policy, there is no transfer for value because of the combined impact of Section 101(a)(2)(A) and Section 1041. The three year rule is avoided because the transfer from the insured to the spouse was for valuable consideration which is an exception to Section 2035 and the transfer by the spouse to the trust or the children is not subject to Section 2035 since it only applies to transfers by insureds.

Section 1041 also applies to transfers of property from one spouse to a trust for the benefit of the other spouse. However, the transfer of basis does not work if the liabilities assumed or the liabilities to which the property is subject exceed the basis of the property transferred to the trust. IRC Section 1041(e). Thus, if an insurance policy is purchased from the insured by a trust for the benefit of the insured's spouse, the exception to the transfer for value rule will not be applicable if a loan against the policy exceeds the insured's basis in the policy.

If the policy is transferred from one corporation to another corporation in a tax-free reorganization, there is no transfer for value since the basis in the hands of the second corporation is determined by reference to the basis in the hands of the first corporation. Reg. Sec. 1.101-1(b)(5), Ex. (2).

(b) Transfer to the Insured. The statute expressly excepts from the transfer for value rule the transfer of the policy to the insured. Also, if the policy is transferred to a grantor trust of which the insured is treated as the owner under IRC

Sections 671 through 677, the transfer of the policy will be treated as if it were transferred to the insured but only to the extent that the insured-grantor is treated as the owner of the trust property. *Swanson v. Commissioner*, 518 F.2d 59 (8th Cir. 1975) where the insured was grantor of 91% of the trust.

(c) Transfer to a Partner of the Insured or to a Partnership in Which the Insured is a Partner. These are very useful exceptions in connection with funding various partnership purchase arrangements. Thus, partners may purchase existing policies on other partners' lives (whether from the partnership, the insured, another partner, or someone else) without fear of transfer for value in order to fund a cross-purchase arrangement. Likewise, a partnership can purchase an insurance policy on a partner's life for the purpose of funding an entity purchase without a transfer for value. However, the transferee partnership must be intended to be and be actually operated as a viable partnership in order to fall within the exception. *Swanson v. Commissioner*, 518 F.2d 59 (8th Cir. 1975). The statutory exception would apply to a transfer for consideration to a person who is a partner of the insured even though the transfer had nothing to do with the partnership.

(d) Transfer to Corporation in Which The Insured is a Shareholder or Officer. Unlike the partner/partnership exceptions, this exception to the transfer for value rule only works one way. If the policy is transferred (whether by the insured, another shareholder or someone else) to a corporation of which the insured is an officer or shareholder, there is no transfer for value. However, if the corporation should transfer the policy to a non-insured stockholder or to a member of the insured's family, there would be a transfer for value. *Monroe v. Patterson*, 197 F.Supp. 146 (N.D. Ala. 1961). *Estate of Rath v. United States*, 608 F.2d 254

(6th Cir. 1979). Also, if the insured is only a director or employee of the corporation but not an officer or a shareholder, the exception does not apply. Can the exception apply if the insured is a nominal officer or only owns one share of stock in the company? Since neither the statute nor the regulation defines officer or shareholder, there is a risk in relying upon this transfer for value exception if the insured performs little or no duties as an officer or owns an insignificant portion of the stock, particularly if the appointment as an officer or the transfer of the stock was in connection with the transfer of the insurance policy to the corporation.

This exception is not nearly as flexible in connection with corporate purchase arrangements as the partner/partnership exceptions. A transfer of policies to a corporation to finance a deferred compensation, stock redemption or some other financial contract with the insured is protected. However, a transfer of corporate owned insurance to a non-insured stockholder or transfer of a policy from one shareholder to another non-insured shareholder for purposes of a cross-purchase agreement would not be protected.

(e) Series of Transfers. If an insurance policy previously tainted under the transfer for value rule is transferred by gift by the original transferee to another, the policy remains tainted despite the second gratuitous transfer. Reg. Sec. 1.101-1(b)(2). However, if a policy previously tainted by a transfer for value is subsequently transferred to the insured, a partner of the insured, a partnership in which the insured is a partner or a corporation in which the insured is an officer or a shareholder, then the taint is removed and the general rule of exclusion of death proceeds from gross income will be applicable. Reg. Sec. 1.101-1(b)(3)(ii).

e. Exception for Policies Owned by Qualified Employee Benefit Plans. If an insurance policy is purchased by a qualified annuity plan described in Section 403(a) or by an employee benefit trust described in IRC Section 401(a) which is exempt from tax under Section 501(a), the proceeds at the death of the insured in excess of the cash surrender value of the policy is not includable in the gross income of the beneficiary as provided in IRC Section 101(a) if the proceeds are paid directly or indirectly from the plan or trust to the beneficiary. IRC Section 72(m)(3)(C). Thus, an amount equal to the cash surrender value will be considered a taxable distribution from the employee benefit plan. *See* item 11 for a more detailed discussion of life insurance in qualified benefit plans.

f. Exception for Proceeds Received by the Insured's Creditor. If an insurance policy is pledged or assigned to a creditor of the owner of the policy, amounts received by the creditor from the proceeds at the death of the insured are not protected by Section 101(a). Reg. Sec. 1.101-1(b)(4). Instead, the proceeds are considered as payment for the underlying debt and are taxable to the creditor in the same manner as such payments would have been taxed without the use of insurance proceeds. Rev. Rul. 70-254, 1970-1 C.B. 31. If the creditor has received a tax deduction for charging off the debt as worthless, then the subsequent collection of the debt from proceeds of the insurance policy will be includable in his income. *St. Louis Refrigerating & Cold Storage Co. v. United States*, 162 F.2d 394 (8th Cir. 1947).

If the creditor has assumed full ownership of the policy in discharge of the basic debt because of the bankruptcy or insolvency of the debtor, the creditor relationship has ended and the former creditor now has an interest in the insurance policy which is subject to the provisions of Section 101. However, the transfer of full ownership to the former creditor would be a transfer for value with the result that the subsequent insurance proceeds would be includable in the former creditor's gross income to the extent it exceeded the cash surrender value of the policy at the date of transfer and premium payments made after that date. *Federal National Bank of Shawnee*, 16 T.C. 54 (1951). However, if the former creditor fell within one of the exceptions of Section 101(a)(2), then the transfer for value rules could be avoided. If a person owns an insurance policy on the life of someone who owes him a debt, the creditor exception to the exclusion from such person's gross income of the insurance proceeds will apply only if the insurance proceeds are received for the purpose of satisfying the debt. Thus, where a company owned a policy on the life of a distributor of its products which was payable to the company entirely and unconditionally at death without regard to a specific debt, the insurance proceeds were excluded from the company's gross income at the distributor's death even though he owed $48,000 in accounts receivable at such time. *L.C. Thomsen & Sons, Inc. v. United States*, 484 F.2d 954 (7th Cir. 1973).

g. Exception Where Proceeds Are Received as Shareholder Dividends or Employee Compensation. Where the insured was an employee or a shareholder of a corporation, the receipt of proceeds at the death of the insured may be treated as compensation or a dividend from the corporation, depending upon who is the owner, beneficiary or premium payer under the policy.

(1) Corporation Owner, Beneficiary and Premium Payer. If the employer is the owner, pays the premium and is the beneficiary under the policy and uses the proceeds received at the death of the insured to discharge a deferred compensation contract in favor of the employee's beneficiaries or as a distribution to the shareholders of the employer, the initial receipt of proceeds by the employer will be tax free under Section 101(a)(1) but the subsequent distribution would be taxable as compensation or dividends, respectively, to the recipients. *Essenfeld v. Commissioner*, 311 F.2d 208 (2nd Cir. 1962). Rev. Rul. 71-79, 1971-1 C.B. 112.

(2) Corporation Owner and Premium Payer. Where the corporation owns the policies and pays the premium but the proceeds are payable to shareholders or to the successors of the insured-shareholder, the IRS takes the position that the proceeds so paid are dividends, since the corporation had all incidents of ownership in the policy and paid the premium. Rev. Rul. 61-134, 1961-2 C.B. 250. The same conclusion was reached by a court of appeals where the

corporation owned the policies and paid the premiums, but the proceeds were payable to a trust for the benefit of the shareholders. *Golden v. Commissioner*, 113 F.2d 590 (3rd Cir. 1940). However, the Sixth Circuit Court of Appeal concluded that insurance proceeds payable directly to the beneficiary of an insured-shareholder under a policy owned by the corporation with premiums paid by the corporation were not dividends, since the distribution was made by the insurance company and not the corporation. The Sixth Circuit distinguished the *Golden* case on the grounds that the actual distribution of proceeds to the stockholders was through a trust created for their benefit by the corporation. *Ducros v. Commissioner*, 272 F.2d 49 (6th Cir. 1959). The IRS has expressly refused to follow the *Ducros* decision. Rev. Rul. 61-134, *supra*.

Presumably, the IRS would take the position that the beneficiaries have received compensation when the proceeds of a corporate-owned policy are payable to the beneficiaries of an employee who was not a shareholder. It should be noted that the *Ducros* court stated that it did not consider the right of the government to tax the premiums paid as dividends to the insured shareholder during his lifetime or to tax the cash surrender value of the policy as dividends to the beneficiaries at the insured shareholder's death, since those issues had not been raised by the government.

Thus, in situations where the corporation owns the policy and pays the premium, the question is whether the proceeds are dividends when paid to a third party as argued by the IRS or whether the premium payments are dividends to the insured shareholder, with the proceeds of the policy being received tax free. One Tax Court decision held that the entire premium payment was not a dividend to the insured shareholder, but suggested *in dicta* that there might be P.S. 58 cost dividend income to the shareholder based upon the amount of insurance coverage benefiting the insured's beneficiary. *Ruth C. Rodebaugh*, 33 T.C.M. 169 (1974). If only the P.S. 58 cost is a dividend rather than the entire premium, perhaps at the death of the insured shareholder, an amount of the proceeds equal to the cash surrender value of the policy immediately before the insured's death (reduced by the aggregate amount of P.S. 58 cost dividend income) would be a dividend based on an analogy with split dollar life insurance discussed in item 10.

(3) Corporation Premium Payer Only. If the employee/shareholder owns the policy and designates the beneficiary, then the proceeds payable upon the insured's death will not be dividends or compensation but will be tax free under Section 101(a)(1). *Doran v. Commissioner*, 246 F.2d 934 (9th Cir. 1957). As noted in item 6.b., the IRS has taken the position that the premium payments by the corporation in such a situation will constitute dividends to the various shareholders who are owners and beneficiaries of the policies. Rev. Rul. 59-184, 1959-1 C.B. 65. Using the analogy of the estate tax regulations which impute to the controlling shareholder the incidents of ownership over any insurance proceeds payable to someone other than the controlled corporation which owns the policy on the insured shareholder's life, the Tax Court has concluded that the receipt of proceeds by the widow of the insured controlling shareholder of the company owning the insurance policy and paying the premiums did not constitute receipt of dividends. *Estate of J.E. Horne*, 65 T.C. 1020 (1975), *acq.* in result, 1980-1 C.B. 1. Thus, in effect, the Tax Court has concluded that, for income tax purposes, the controlling shareholder is the real owner of any insurance policy owned by his controlled corporation, at least to the extent that proceeds are payable to someone other than the corporation.

3. Cash Value Growth in Life Insurance Contract

a. General rule of non-taxability. As a general rule, the annual increases in the cash surrender value of a life insurance policy are not currently taxable to the policy owner. For policies issued after 1984, this is the result of IRC Section 7702(g). There is no express statutory exclusion from gross income for cash value increases in policies issued before 1985. This is true even for pre-1985 flexible premium policies. IRC Section 101(f) only mentions the exclusion of the death proceeds from gross income for policies meeting the alternative tests specified by that Section. However, pre-1985 case law makes it clear that there is no constructive receipt to the policy owner of increases in cash value since access to it would require the substantial restriction of total or partial surrender of the policy. *Theodore H. Cohen,* 39 T.C. 1055 (1965), acq. 1964-1 C.B. 4. *Abram Nesbitt, II,* 43 T.C. 629 (1965).

b. Exception for Failure to Meet Definition of Life Insurance Contract. As noted earlier, if a post-1984 life insurance contract is disqualifed under IRC Section 7702 or a variable life insurance contract is disqualified under the diversified investment provisions of IRC Section 817(h), the Code treats such a disqualified policy as a combined term insurance policy and an investment fund with the income portion of the investment fund being currently taxable to the policy owner. IRC Section 7702(g). Section 101(f) does not state what the current tax consequences are for a pre-1985 flexible premium policy which fails both of the tests specified in that Section. Of course, there is no statutory provision concerning a pre-1985 non-flexible premium policy which fails to meet the judicial requirements of risk-shifting and risk-distribution.

For disqualified pre-1985 policies, the IRS and the courts have several theories available concerning the income taxation of increases of cash surrender value of such policies. First, they might apply the same rules embodied in Section 7702 discussed below. A second alternative is to treat the policy as two separate contracts -- a deferred annuity and a term life insurance policy with the cash value of the annuity used to pay the insurance premiums. In such a case, distributions from the reserve to pay premiums (or otherwise paid to the policy owner) would be subject to the provisions of IRC Section 72(e), under which distributions and loans before the annuity starting date are first taken from the income accumulated in the contract but such accumulated income would not be taxed until either distributed or borrowed. A third approach is to treat the cash value as a premium deposit or advance premium account, with the result that the interest earned on the cash value will be taxed to the policy owner as the premiums are paid. Rev. Rul. 66-120, 1966-1 C.B.

14. A fourth possibility is to treat the cash value of the disqualified policy as an interest bearing side fund used to pay premiums in which case all interest on the fund will be currently taxed to the owner. Rev. Rul. 66-120, *supra*. P.L.R. 8047051.

What happens to a post-1984 policy that fails to meet either test under Section 7702? The Code treats such a disqualified policy as a combined term insurance policy and an investment fund. IRC Section 7702(g)(2). Income on a disqualified contract will be taxable to the policyholder as ordinary income each year and the constructive receipt rules are waived. Once a policy is disqualified, it will remain disqualified even though it might meet the test requirements in a future year. If a qualified contract becomes disqualified, income on the contract for prior years is treated as received in a lump sum during the first year of disqualification. "Income on the contract" for a taxable year includes the increase in net surrender value (determined with regard to surrender charges but not with regard to policy loans) of the policy during the taxable year plus the cost of life insurance protection during such year less premiums paid during the year. The cost of the life insurance protection during a taxable year is based upon the lesser of the uniform premium table (based on 5-year age brackets) to be prescribed by regulations or the mortality charge, if any, stated in the contract. In the case of the death of the insured under a disqualified contract, the death benefit paid in excess of the net surrender charge is exempt from tax. Presumably, the portion of the net surrender charge taxable in previous years as "income on the contract" will not be taxed again since it now forms a basis in the contract.

There are several exceptions to the rule that an insurance contract which fails to meet one of the two tests is disqualified. First, the Secretary of Treasury can waive disqualification if the failure to meet one of the tests was due to reasonable error and reasonable steps are being taken to remedy the error. Second, a premium payment in excess of the guideline premium limitation will not disqualify the policy if the premium is needed to prevent termination of the policy and if the policy would have no cash surrender value at the end of the extension period. Third, as noted earlier, there is no disqualification for premium payments made in excess of the guideline premium requirements if the excess amount (with interest) is returned as a reduction of premium within 60 days of the end of the contract year but the interest will be includible in the policyholder's gross income.

c. Exception for Dividends and Withdrawals From or Cancellation and Surrender of Policy.

(1) Dividends. As a general rule, dividends received on a participating life insurance contract are considered to be a return of premiums and will not be includible in the gross income of the policyholder until, in the aggregate with previous non-taxable distributions from the policy, the dividends exceed all of the premiums or other consideration paid. Reg. Sec. 1.72-11(b)(1). This rule applies to dividends received in cash, used to purchase paid-up additions or used to purchase a term insurance rider on the policy. If the dividend is left with the insurance company to accumulate at interest, the dividend is not taxable but the interest would be includible in the gross income of the policy owner under the doctrine of constructive receipt if there were no restrictions upon his right to withdraw such interest. *Theodore H. Cohen*, 39 T.C. 1055 (1963) acq. 1964-1 C.B. 4. If the dividends plus the aggregate previous distributions from the policy exceed the premium investment in the policy, the dividend would be includible in the gross income of the policy owner. IRC Section 72(e)(5)(A) and (C). However, in regard to federal government National Service Life Insurance, all dividends (paid in cash, accumulated or used to purchase paid-up additions) are exempt from income inclusion without regard to previous premium payments but any interest on accumulated dividends subject to withdrawal are included in the policyholder's gross income. Rev. Rul. 57-441, 1957-2 C.B. 45. Rev. Rul. 71-306, 1971-2 C.B. 76. Rev. Rul. 72-604, 1972-2 C.B. 35. For special income tax rules for dividends which benefit the employee in a split dollar arrangement, *see* item 10.

(2) Withdrawal. As a general rule, a withdrawal from the cash reserves of a flexible premium

policy will not result in inclusion in the gross income of the policy owner unless the aggregate previous withdrawals and tax-free distributions from the policy exceed the accumulated premiums and other consideration paid for the contract. If the aggregate withdrawals and other distributions do exceed the consideration paid, the current withdrawal would be includible in income to the extent there was accumulated income contained in the cash surrender value. IRC Section 72(e)(5)(A).

However, there is an exception to this general rule in certain cases where there is a cash distribution within the first fifteen years after the policy has been issued accompanied by a reduction in the death benefits under the policy. IRC Section 7702(f)(7). If this should occur, then the "premium first" rule of Section 72(e)(5) is inapplicable and the cash distribution will be deemed to bring out accumulated income in the cash surrender value but not in excess of a statutory recapture ceiling under Section 7702(f)(7). There are separate statutory ceiling tests applied if the cash distribution occurs within the first five years after issuance of the contract or after the first five years from such issuance and, if the cash distribution is within the first five years, there is a separate test for whole life policies which originally qualified as life insurance contracts under the cash value accumulation test and for flexible premium policies which originally qualified as life insurance contracts under the guideline premium-cash value corridor test. IRC Section 7702(f)(7)(C) and (D). Any cash distributions within two years before a reduction in death benefit is deemed to be in connection with the future death benefit reduction and the Treasury Secretary is authorized to cover additional anticipatory distributions by regulation. IRC Section 7702(f)(7)(E).

This new fifteen year rule applies only to policies issued after 1984. Withdrawals from a life insurance contract will not result in inclusion in income of the policyholder to the extent of accumulated income in the cash value of the policy unless the withdrawal is within the first fifteen years of the policy and runs afoul of the recapture ceiling test. Since loans against the cash value of insurance policies are not treated as distributions and do not reduce the death benefits, loans are not subject to the provisions of Section 7702(f)(7).

(3) Redemption, Surrender or Maturity. Any amount received in a single sum under a life insurance contract on its complete surrender, redemption or maturity will be includible in the gross income of the policy owner to the extent such amount exceeds the investment in the contract. IRC Section 72(e)(5)(A) and (E). Reg. Sec. 1.72-11(d)(1). If the policy owner elects within sixty days after the day on which a lump sum would be payable upon the surrender, redemption or maturity of the life insurance contract to receive an annuity in lieu of the lump sum, the constructive receipt rules will not apply and the excess of the cash surrender value over the investment in the contract will not be included in the gross income of the policy owner at that time. The option exercised within the sixty-day period must be to receive an annuity which is payable in periodic installments at regular intervals over a period of more than one full year. Reg. Sec. 1.72-12. Reg. Sec. 1.72-2(b)(2). If the option is exercised timely, the payments upon the surrender, redemption or maturity of the life insurance contract will be taxed under the annuity rules under IRC Section 72(b). Thus, if the annuity option is exercised after the expiration of the sixty-day period, the excess of the cash value of the policy over the investment in the policy will be ordinary income in the year of surrender, redemption or maturity even though the payments are received in installments.

If a settlement option is exercised to receive payment in lieu of a lump sum in a form other than annuity (e.g., retention of proceeds and payment of interest only), the sixty day provision is inapplicable and the settlement option must be exercised prior to the surrender, redemption or maturity date in order to prevent constructive receipt of the proceeds. *Constance C. Frackelton,* 46 B.T.A. 883

(1942). However, even though the interest only option is elected prior to the maturity date, if the policy owner retains the right to withdraw the proceeds on any interest payment date, he has constructive receipt of the entire proceeds on any such interest date and will be taxed on the excess of the cash surrender value over the investment in the contract. *Blum v. Higgins*, 150 F.2d 471 (2nd Cir. 1945). Even when a timely interest-only option is exercised, the interest payments will be included in gross income. IRC Section 72(j). However, the interest payments will be includible in gross income only when they are received even though the option allows the interest payments to accrue if the policyholder does not have a contractual right to withdraw the payments. *Fleming v. Commissioner*, 241 F.2d 78 (5th Cir. 1957).

(4) <u>Investment in Contract</u>. Whether dividends, withdrawals or proceeds upon the surrender, redemption or maturity of a policy are involved, it is important to know what the taxpayer's investment in the insurance contract is in order to determine the amount includible in his gross income.

The Internal Revenue Code defines investment in the contract as the aggregate amount of premiums or other consideration paid for the contract less the aggregate amount received under the contract to the extent previously excludible from gross income. IRC Section 72(c)(1). IRC Section 72(e)(6). Thus, the starting point is the aggregate premiums paid by the taxpayer plus any other consideration paid if an existing policy had been purchased by the taxpayer. This amount will be reduced by any dividends previously received, any unrepaid loans, any accumulated interest on loans and any other amounts received which were not previously included in gross income (e.g., withdrawals). Reg. Sec. 1.72-6(a)(1).

Clearly, if dividends are received in cash or are used to reduce premiums, they will reduce the investment in the contract. Presumably, dividends used to purchase term riders will also reduce the investment in the contract but dividends used to purchase paid-up additions would not since they will be retained within the policy as part of the cash value of the paid-up additions. Any portion of total premiums paid which is attributable to other benefits, such as disability income, waiver of premium or accidental death protection, also reduce investment in contracts. Rev. Rul. 55-359, 1955 C.B. 323. See *Estate of Wong Wing Non*, 18 T.C. 205 (1952). The *Wong Wing Non* case also held that premiums paid on a policy pursuant to a disability waiver provision in the contract could not be counted as premiums paid by the insured for purposes of determining his basis in the contract. Interest paid on premium loans is not consideration paid for a policy and do not increase the policy owner's basis. *Chapin v. McGowan*, 271 F.2d 856 (2nd Cir. 1959). In addition, an employee's basis or investment in his life insurance contract is increased by any P.S. 58 cost income realized from policies held by a qualified pension or profit sharing plan. Reg. Sec. 1.72-16(b)(4). Presumably, the same would be true for P.S. 58 cost income realized by an employee under a split dollar life insurance arrangement. See P.L.R. 8310027.

d. <u>Single Premium and Modified Endowment Contracts</u>. Soon after the passage of the TRA 1986, Congress became concerned with the marketing of certain single premium insurance policies as tax shelter investment vehicles. Some policies were being issued with the minimum amount of pure insurance coverage necessary to meet the statutory definition of life insurance contract and with the single premium being increased by estimating mortality charges and other policy expenses in excess of the experience of the insurance company involved. Policyholders were encouraged to annually withdraw from or borrow against the policy an amount equal to the cash value increase during that year with interest charges for the loans being almost completely offset by the income credited to the cash value subject to the loans. Since, under Section 72(e)(5), withdrawals were taken from the premium payments rather than income build-up and loans were not considered distributions at all, the practical effect was that the policyholder enjoyed an amount equal to the income produced by the policy cash value each year without income tax consequences.

As noted earlier, in TAMRA, Congress incorporated into the definition of life insurance contract a requirement that reasonable mortality and expense charges be used in meeting the two alternative definitional tests effective for contracts entered into on or after October 21, 1988. IRC Section 7702(c)(3)(B). In addition, effective for contracts purchased on or after June 21, 1988, Congress generally imposed the taxation rules for deferred annuities on certain single premium contracts classified as modified endowment contracts under IRC Section 7702A.

(1) Definition of Modified Endowment Contract. A modified endowment contract is an insurance policy in which the cumulative premium payments in any one of the first seven contract years exceeds the sum of the net level premiums which would have been paid to provide a paid-up policy after the payment of seven level annual premiums (the "7-pay test"). IRC Section 7702A. The 7-pay test is calculated by using the computation under the cash value accumulation test in determining the definition of a life insurance contract. The calculations are based on the initial death benefit ignoring future changes.

The computation of the 7-pay test premium may be increased in two situations. For policies with initial death benefit of $10,000 or less (all policies issued by the same insurance company on the same insured are aggregated), the 7-pay premiums will be increased by an expense charge of $75 each year if the policy requires at least seven non-decreasing annual payments. IRC Section 7702A(c)(4). In addition, the Secretary of Treasury may issue regulations for taking into account expenses solely attributable to the collection of premiums paid more frequently than annually (particularly for small policies). IRC Section 7702A(c)(5).

If there is a reduction in death benefit during the first seven years, the 7-pay test is recalculated for the first seven years using the reduced death benefit. IRC Section 7702A(c)(2). However, a reduction in benefits attributable to non-payment of premiums shall not cause a recalculation if the benefits are reinstated within 90 days after such reduction. IRC Section 7702A(c)(2)(B). If premiums in excess of the 7-pay test for any year are paid, the modified endowment contract rules will not apply if such premium payments with interest thereon are returned within sixty days after the end of the policy year. However, any such return interest will be includible in the taxpayer's gross income. IRC Section 7702A(e). If a modified endowment contract is exchanged for another policy, the new policy is also a modified endowment contract. IRC Section 7702A(a)(2).

(2) Material Changes. If there is a material change in benefits or other terms of an insurance policy, the 7-pay test will be applied as if this were a new contract at the date of the material change. IRC Section 7702A(c)(3). The Senate Committee Report as adopted by the Conference Agreement states that a decrease in death benefit is not a material change. An increase in future benefits under the contract will be a material change unless the increase is attributable to (1) the payment of premiums necessary to fund the lowest death benefit payable in the first seven contract years or (2) the purchase of paid-up additions with policy dividends. In addition, the Secretary of Treasury is authorized to issue regulations which would treat any cost of living increase in death benefits based on an established broad-base index as not being a material change if such increase is funded ratably over the remaining life of the insurance contract. Other increases in benefits (e.g., option 2 universal life insurance) would result in material changes. In applying the 7-pay test to a policy after a material change, appropriate adjustments are to be made for the cash surrender value (IRC Section 7702A(c)(3)(A)(ii)) and the Conference Committee Report states that each 7-pay premium will be reduced by a portion of the cash value at the date of material change equal to the 7-pay premium for future policy benefits divided by a net single premium for such benefits.

(3) Distributions from Modified Endowment Contracts. When a life insurance policy fails the 7-pay test and becomes a modified endowment

policy, distributions from such policy are subject to the same rules as distributions from deferred annuity contracts. Accumulated cash value income rather than premiums come out first with withdrawals and distributions. IRC Section 72(e)(10). Loans against the cash value of a modified endowment contract or from the pledge of such contract are treated as distributions. The Conference Committee Report states that dividends retained by the insurance carrier to pay premiums (including the purchase of paid-up additions) will not be considered distributions. However, all other dividends (including dividends used to reduce previous loans against the policy) will be distributions. Furthermore, loans against the policy to pay a premium or interest on a prior loan will be considered a distribution. If a policy fails to meet the 7-pay test because of a reduction of death benefits during the first seven years or because of a subsequent material change, the special income tax rules for a modified endowment contract will apply for distributions during the contract year in which the 7-pay test is not met, all future distributions from such contract and all distributions within two years before the failure to meet the 7-pay test. In addition, the Secretary of Treasury may issue regulations to cover distributions in previous years which were made in anticipation of such failure to meet the 7-pay test. IRC Section 7702(A)(d).

In order to stop the marketing of serial contracts that are designed to avoid the distribution rules, all modified endowment contracts issued by the same insurance company to the same policyholder during any twelve month period are treated as one modified endowment contract and the Secretary of Treasury is authorized to issue regulations to provide additional rules to prevent avoidance of the distribution tax through serial purchases of contracts or otherwise. IRC Section 72(e)(11).

(4) <u>Ten Percent Additional Tax</u>. The portion of any distribution from a modified endowment contract which is includible in the policy owner's income is subject to an additional ten percent income tax. IRC Section 72(v). Exceptions to this ten

percent additional tax are made for distributions after the taxpayer attains 59-1/2 years of age, becomes disabled, or receives the distribution as part of a series of substantially equal periodic payments (not less frequently than annually) made for the life (or life expenctancy) of the taxpayer or the joint lives (or joint life expectancies) of such taxpayer and his beneficiary. Exceptions to the distribution rules are made for loans against or pledges of a modified endowment contract with a maximum death benefit not in excess of $25,000 for the payment of burial expenses or pre-arranged funeral expenses. IRC Section 72(e)(10)(B).

(5) <u>Effective Date and Grandfather Rules</u>. Generally, the modified endowment contract rules apply to contracts entered into on or after June 21, 1988. Presumably, this would include a contract issued on or after such date even though it is in exchange for a contract issued prior to June 21, 1988. There is an exception to the general rule that a new contract received in exchange for a modified endowment contract is itself a modified endowment contract. If the modified endowment contract is entered into on or after June 21, 1988 but before November 10, 1988, it may be exchanged before February 10, 1989, for a contract which meets the 7-pay test if gain (if any) is recognized by the taxpayer on the exchange.

A grandfathered life insurance contract may become subject to the 7-pay test if any of the following material changes occur: (1) A term life insurance contract is exchanged for a whole life policy, (2) the death benefit under the policy is increased or a qualified additional benefit is increased or added on or after June 21, 1988 and, before June 21, 1988, the owner of the contract did not have a unilateral right under the contract to obtain such increase or addition without providing additional evidence of insurability, or (3) the death benefit under the grandfathered contract as of October 20, 1988, increases by more than $150,000 unless the policy as of June 21, 1988, required at least seven annual level premium payments and the policyholder continues to make such level annual premium payments (the typical whole life insurance contract).

4. Exchange of Life Insurance Contracts.

Exchanges of older insurance policies for new policies which pay higher rates of return on cash values have become very popular in recent years. It is important that the exchange of these policies qualify for tax-free treatment under IRC Section 1035 or else the surrender proceeds from the older policy will constitute ordinary income to the extent they exceed the policy owner's basis.

a. IRC Section 1035. No gain or loss is recognized on the exchange of a life insurance contract for a life insurance, endowment or annuity contract. However, non-recognition is not granted to a reverse exchange of an endowment or an annuity contract for a life insurance contract. Reg. Sec. 1.1035-1. The same regulation requires that the exchanged contracts involve the same insured (but not necessarily the same owner). It should be observed that the same non-recognition rules apply to the exchange of an annuity contract for an annuity contract since most of the rulings in this area involves such exchanges and will be cited as support for similar questions involving exchanges of life insurance contracts. IRC Section 1035(a)(3). As long as the same insured is involved, different insurance carriers can be involved in the same exchange. Rev. Rul. 73-124, 1973-1 C.B. 200. Also, the exchange of one type of life insurance contract for another (e.g., fixed premium for flexible premium) should fall within the parameters of Section 1035. *See* Rev. Rul. 68-235, 1968-1 C.B. 360 where the exchange of a standard annuity for a variable annuity was approved.

b. What is an "Exchange"? The vast majority of the IRS rulings in this area have involved the exchange of annuities but the same principles should be applicable to the exchange of life insurance contracts except to the extent noted. There are two basic procedures which could be used in the exchange of life insurance contracts -- the inside procedure and the outside procedure.

The "inside procedure" involves the assignment of the life insurance contract to a second insurance company which surrenders the old policy to the first insurance company and issues a new policy purchased from the surrender proceeds. This is the procedure favored by the Internal Revenue Service. *See* Rev. Rul. 72-358, 1972-2 C.B. 473, where the inside procedure of the exchange of a life insurance contract for a varible annuity contract was approved. The inside procedure is not possible where the exchange involves IRC Section 403(b) annuities or annuities which have come out of qualified plans, since both are required to be non-transferrable under IRC Section 401(g). In this situation, the IRS has ruled that a tax-free exchange can take place where the employee enters into a pre-existing binding agreement with his or her employer to endorse the surrender check to the employer who will then purchase the second annuity. Rev. Rul. 73-124, 1973-1 C.B. 200. Tax-free treatment has also been granted where the pre-existing binding agreement concerning the non-transferrable annuity is between the employee and the second insurance company. P.L.R. 8526038. Presumably, since life insurance contracts are not subject to the non-transferability rules of Section 401(g), the "binding agreement" exception to the inside procedure is probably not available as is the case for transferrable annuities. *See* P.L.R. 8515063 and P.L.R. 8741052.

Under the "outside procedure", the policyholder surrenders the old contract and immediately uses the proceeds to purchase a new contract from a second insurance carrier. The IRS does not favor the outside procedure and has denied non-recognition of gain even where the surrender proceeds check was either payable directly to the second insurance carrier or was immediately endorsed over to that carrier. P.L.R. 8310033. P.L.R. 8515063. The Tax Court has disagreed with the IRS and has allowed the use of the outside procedure for the exchange of Section 403(b) annuities where the surrender proceeds check was endorsed directly to the second carrier even without a binding agreement. *Martin I. Greene*, 85 T.C. 1024 (1985).

Despite the favorable *Greene* decision, the safest course of action for the exchange of life insurance contracts is the use of the inside procedure. Although the IRS has acquiesed in the *Greene* decision (1986-2 C.B. 1), the acquiesence was in the results only, indicating disagreement with some or all of the reasons used in the decision. The IRS preference for the use of the inside procedure has been reaffirmed in P.L.R. 8741052 which was issued after the acquiescence in the *Greene* decision.

c. Exchange of Policy Subject to Loan. If "other property" is received in connection with an otherwise tax-free exchange, any gain contained in the exchanged property will be recognized up to the fair market value of the other property ("boot"). IRC Section 1031(b). However, in the exchange of life insurance contracts, the receipt of boot will first result in a reduction of basis in the policy under Section 72(e)(5)(A) and gain will be taxable only if the fair market value of the boot exceeds the basis in the exchanged policy. If boot is received in connection with an exchange of life insurance contracts, no loss on the transaction will be recognized. IRC Section 1031(c). The gain triggered by boot (or by the total failure of an exchange of policies to qualify for non-recognition of gain) will be ordinary income rather than capital gain, since the transaction would be treated as a partial (or complete) surrender of the policy taxable under Section 72(e)(5)(A) and (E). *See* Rev. Rul. 54-264, 1954-2 C.B. 57.

Liabilities extinguished or assumed in an exchange will be treated as boot, but they will be offset by any liabilities assumed by the other party. Reg. Sec. 1.1031(b)-1(c). Thus, if a life insurance policy subject to a loan against cash value is exchanged for a new policy, the extinguishment of the loan upon the exchange will be treated as boot and will be taxed if it exceeds the basis in the exchanged contract, to the extent gain has accumulated in the policy. However, if a policy with indebtedness is exchanged for another policy with an identical amount of indebtedness, there is no boot. P.L.R. 8604033. P.L.R. 8816015. If it is not possible to exchange a policy subject to indebtedness for a new policy subject to an identical amount of indebtedness, one way of avoiding boot is to pay off the loan on the old policy, exchange it for the new policy and then borrow against the new policy, if necessary.

d. Exchange Gain and Basis. In a tax-free exchange, the new policy will have the same basis to the taxpayer as his basis in the old policy decreased by any boot received and increased by any amount of gain recognized in the exchange. IRC Section 1031(d). If boot other than money or extinguishment of liabilities is received, the basis must be proportioned between the insurance contract and such boot. Reg. Section 1.1031(b)-1(c).

e. <u>Tax-Free Exchanges and Various Grandfather Provisions</u>. The definition of "life insurance contract" contained in IRC Section 7702 applies to all insurance contracts issued after 1984. If a pre-1985 contract is exchanged for a post-1984 contract, the grandfathering is lost and the provisions of Section 7702 will apply. P.L.R. 8816015.

The Section 264(a)(3) limitation upon the deductibility of interest incurred on an indebtedness to purchase a life insurance contract applies only to contracts purchased after August 6, 1963. If a pre-August 7, 1963 contract is exchanged for a post-August 6, 1963, the grandfather exclusion is lost. P.L.R. 8816015.

Does the "4 out of 7 rule" qualification of the old policy carry over to the new policy after the exchange for interest deduction purposes under Section 264(c)(1)? Although not ruling on this point, the IRS has stated that the basis of the old policy carries over to the new policy after a Section 1035 exchange since the new contract is treated as a "continuation" of the old contract. P.L.R. 8604033. This language gave hope that, if the new policy is a continuation of the old, then tacking for purposes of the 4 out of 7 rule would be permissible and that the new contract would not have to requalify for the interest deduction. However, the anti-grandfathering ruling of P.L.R. 8816015 has thrown a considerable damper on this expectation although the issues are not the same.

If a life insurance contract which is grandfathered from the 7-pay test because it was issued before June 21, 1988 is exchanged on or after June 21, 1988, the grandfathering is lost and the new policy must qualify under the 7-pay test to avoid being a modified endowment contract. *See* H. Rept. 100-795, pp. 480 and 482.

If a modified endowment contract is exchanged for another policy, the new policy is also a modified endowment contract. IRC Section 7702A(a)(2).

If a modified endowment contract is entered into on or after June 21, 1988 but before November 11, 1988, it may be exchanged before February 11, 1989 for a contract which meets the 7-pay test if gain (if any) is recognized by the taxpayer on the exchange. TAMRA, Section 5012(e)(4).

5. Deductibility of Premium Payments on Insurance Policies.

   a. Personally owned life insurance. Any premiums paid by the insured on a personally owned life insurance policy are considered a personal expense and therefore are not deductible on the insured's income tax return. Reg. Sec. 1.262-1(b)(1). *John A. Guglielmetti*, 35 T.C. 668 (1961). Furthermore, premiums paid by a non-insured owner on a life insurance policy are not deductible under IRC Sec. 265, relating to expenses allocable to tax-exempt income. If such a deduction was allowed, there would result a double benefit to the taxpayer under the tax laws -- deduction for the premium paid and no taxes paid on the death proceeds. Reg. Sec. 1.264-1(a). *Jones v. Commissioner*, 231 F.2d 655 (3rd Cir. 1956).

   b. Business Life Insurance. IRC Section 264(a)(1) provides that no deduction is allowed for premiums paid on any life insurance policy insuring the life of any officer or employee of a taxpayer, or any person financially interested in the taxpayer's business, if the taxpayer is either directly or indirectly a beneficiary under the policy. Under Reg. Sec. 1.264-1(a), any such premiums will still not be deductible even though they otherwise may have been deductible as ordinary and necessary business expenses of the taxpayer. Regardless of whether the taxpayer is named as the beneficiary of the proceeds, no deduction for the premiums will be allowed if the taxpayer reserved any incidents of ownership over the policy or some other beneficial interest such as the right to change beneficiaries, the right to receive any cash surrender value of the policy, the right to make loans against the cash surrender value, or the right to attach the proceeds of a policy held in trust. Rev. Rul. 66-203, 1966-2 C.B. 104. Rev. Rul. 70-148, 1970-1 C.B. 60. Independent of any IRC Section 264 considerations, premium payments made by a corporation on an insurance policy on a shareholder's life designed to fund a stock purchase agreement are not deductible as ordinary and necessary business expenses since the expenditures are for the acquisition of a capital asset which must be capitalized. Rev. Rul. 70-117, 1970-1 C.B. 30.

Even if the taxpayer is only a partial beneficiary of the policy on an employee's life, the deduction for premiums is disallowed in total and is not adjusted in proportion to the degree of the employer's involvement as a beneficiary under the policy. Rev. Rul. 66-203, 1966-2 C.B. 104. Consequently, with regard to the portion of premiums paid on a split dollar policy by an employer, there is no business deduction for the employer's portion of the annual premium since it is a beneficiary under the policy. In addition, the employer is not allowed to deduct the value of the coverage under the split dollar policy which may be taxable to the employee since the employer has not paid or incurred any expense other than the portion of the nondeductible premium expense which it has paid. Rev. Rul. 64-328, 1964-2 C.B. 11.

A taxpayer is considered a beneficiary under a policy where he, as a principal member of a partnership, takes out an insurance policy on his own life irrevocably designating his partner as the sole beneficiary in order to induce his partner to retain his investment in the partnership. However, if the taxpayer is not a beneficiary under the policy, the premiums so paid will not be disallowed as deductions merely because the taxpayer may derive a benefit from increased efficiency of the officer or the employee insured. Reg. Sec. 1.264-1(b).

(1) Creditor Insurance. When an individual obtains credit, the lending entity may require the debtor either to apply for an insurance policy in the amount of the debt and name the lending entity as beneficiary or to assign an existing policy to the lending entity to assure payment of its debt in the event of the debtor's death. If the debt incurred is personal in nature, the premiums paid by the debtor will not be deductible under IRC Section 262. If the debt is business in nature, the premiums paid by the debtor will not be deductible under IRC Section 264(a)(1) since the debtor would normally be a person financially interested in the business which received the loan and would be an indirect beneficiary of the proceeds because the loan incurred would be paid upon his death.

A creditor who has a collateral assignment of an insurance policy on the debtor's life as a security interest for a business loan may deduct any premiums paid on such policy only if the creditor has no right under local law to recover the premium payments from the debtor (e.g., bankruptcy) and if the cash surrender value of the policy is insufficient to cover the unpaid debt and the premium payment. Such premium payments may constitute ordinary and necessary business expenses incident to the protection of collateral in the usual course of a taxpayer's business under IRC Section 162. However, if the creditor recovers any portion of the premiums it has previously deducted, the recovery will be income. Rev. Rul. 75-46, 1975-1 C.B. 55. The Fourth Circuit Court of Appeals has also allowed the creditor a deduction for premium payments on a policy securing a business debt where the debtor was insolvent but did not require that the cash surrender value be less than the premium payments. *Commissioner v. Charleston National Bank,* 213 F.2d 45 (1954). Another court allowed a similar deduction in a factual situation where the cash value was less than the premiums with no comment as to whether the deductions would have been allowed if the cash value had exceeded the premium payments. *Dominion National Bank,* 26 B.T.A. 421 (1932). Premium payments by a creditor on a policy held as collateral security for a business debt on the life of a bankrupt debtor would be deductible as ordinary and necessary business expenses and not as bad debts. *The First National & Trust Company of Tulsa v. Jones,* 143 F.2d 652 (10th Cir. 1944). However, even in a business debt context, if the borrower is an officer, employee or a person financially interested in the trade or business carried on by the creditor, a deduction would be disallowed under IRC Sec. 264(a)(1). Rev. Rul. 75-46, *supra.*

On the other hand, if a non-business debt is involved, the creditor who has received a collateral assignment of a policy on the life of the debtor as security for such debt may not deduct the premium paid on such policy, even if the debt is worthless and the cash value is insufficient to cover the debt and the premium payment, on the grounds that the payments are a capital investment rather than expenses incurred for the production or collection of income or the management of property held for the production of income. *United States v. Mellinger*, 228 F.2d 688 (5th Cir. 1956). There is an indication in the *Mellinger* decision that the Fifth Circuit might even consider such premium payments in a business context to be a non-deductible capital expenditure rather than an ordinary and necessary business expense, which would be contrary to the position of the courts in *Charleston National Bank, supra* and *First National Bank & Trust Company of Tulsa, supra*. 228 F.2d at 692. In an unusual fact situation, the IRS allowed a deduction for premium payments on a policy on a debtor's life owned by a creditor in the business of selling homesites, where the insurance was in the amount of the unpaid purchase price, there was no separate charge to the purchasers for the insurance coverage and the death proceeds were to be used to retire the balance of the purchase price. Although the premiums were deductible under IRC Section 162(a), the IRS also ruled that the proceeds of the policy were includible in the gross income of the creditor as collections on the unpaid balance of a purchase price rather than the receipt of insurance proceeds. Rev. Rul. 70-254, 1970-1 C.B. 31.

If a creditor has a collateral assignment on an insurance policy to secure a debt which later proves to be worthless, the worthless debt may be deducted, but only to the extent it exceeds the cash surrender value of the policy. *Dominion National Bank*, 26 B.T.A. 421 (1932).

(2) Employee Compensation. An employer can deduct payments paid on insurance coverage on the life of an employee if the employer is not directly or indirectly a beneficiary of the policy, and if the premiums represent additional reasonable compensation for services rendered by the employee. Thus if the employer has no ownership rights or beneficial interest in the policy, and the proceeds are payable to the employee's estate or personal beneficiary, the premiums ordinarily are deductible by the employer as additional compensation to the employee. IRC Section 162(a).

c. <u>Charitable Deduction</u>. If a policy owner assigns an insurance policy to a qualified charity or to a trustee with a charity as an irrevocable beneficary, the amount deductible as a charitable contribution is either the value of the policy or the policy owner's cost basis (i.e., premiums paid), whichever is less. IRC Section 170(e).

If the policy is owned by the charitable entity and the donor is simply paying the premiums for the coverage, those payments would be considered deductible charitable contributions, subject to the overall limits on charitable giving described below. It is unclear whether premium payments made directly to the insurance company to maintain a policy owned by a charity (instead of making cash payments directly to the charity in the amount of the premiums) are gifts "to" the charity or merely gifts "for the use of" the charity. The distinction is important because of the limitation on charitable deduction that the donor can take for income tax purposes in the current year.

An individual is allowed a charitable deduction of up to 50% of his adjusted gross income ("AGI") for any charitable contribution <u>made</u> <u>to</u> a qualifying charitable entity listed under IRC Section 170(b)(1)(A). On the other hand, an individual is allowed a charitable deduction of up to 30% of his AGI for any charitable gift made <u>for</u> <u>the</u> <u>use</u> <u>of</u> such charity or <u>to</u> <u>or</u> <u>for</u> <u>the</u> <u>use</u> <u>of</u> other types of charitable organizations. IRC Section 170(b)(1)(B). This deduction is limited to the lesser of: 30% of the AGI or 50% of the AGI less the amount of contributions made to the original 50% qualifying charities.

There are two possible methods of obtaining a charitable deduction for premium payments for policies owned by a charity. One is to obtain a specific agreement with the charity that any premiums paid directly to the insurance company are made only to that company acting in its capacity as an agent and under the authority to receive contributions on behalf of the charity in the form of premiums being paid. The better solution, if applicable, is to contribute the premium payments directly to the charity which then pays the premiums to the insurance company.

The IRS takes the position that no deduction will be allowed for gifts made after July 31, 1969, involving a split dollar plan in which the donor gives the charity the cash surrender value of a policy and a non-charitable beneficiary takes the balance. A gift of the cash surrender value is considered a gift of less than the entire interest in the property whether the donor retains the right to designate the beneficiary of the risk portion or irrevocably designates the non-charitable beneficiary prior to making the gift. IRC Section 170(f)(3). Rev. Rul. 76-143, 1976-1 C.B. 63.

d. Alimony Deduction. The deductibility as an alimony payment of insurance premiums paid by an insured former spouse on a policy owned by a non-insured former spouse pursuant to a divorce decree or separation agreement may depend upon whether such decree or agreement was rendered or entered into before 1985 or after 1984, since the Tax Reform Act of 1984 substantially changed the alimony laws for income tax purposes.

Basically, after 1984, the following requirements must be met for payments to be treated as alimony: (a) payments must be in cash; (b) payments must be pursuant to a divorce or separation instrument which includes a decree of divorce or separate maintenance or a written instrument incident to such a decree, a written separation agreement, any other decree requiring a spouse to make payments for support or maintenance of the other spouse (e.g., temporary support orders); (c) the spouses do not live in the same household unless the alimony is pursuant to a written separation agreement or temporary support order; (d) payments end at the recipient spouse's death with no substitute payments to the recipient's estate; and (e) the spouses do not file a joint income tax return. IRC Section 71(b) and (e). The House Report on the Tax Reform Act of 1984 stated that amounts payable under a life insurance contract on the life of the recipient spouse will not be treated as a substitute payment which would affect the alimony status of other payments during the recipient's lifetime. H.R. Rept. No. 98-432, Part 2, 98th Cong., 2d Sess. 1496 (1984). However, since the temporary regulations do not mention this exception to the prohibition to substitute payments, there is some question as to whether the IRS will follow the House Report.

In regard to post-1984 instruments, the divorce or separation instrument may expressly exempt payments which would otherwise qualify under the Code as alimony or separate maintenance payments. IRC Section 71(b)(1)(B). The parties to a divorce or separation instrument may have the post-1984 alimony rules apply to a pre-1985 divorce or separation instrument by modifying the old instrument to expressly provide that the new law will apply. Reg. Section 1.71-1T(e), Q/A-26. Consequently, premium payments pursuant to a post-1984 divorce or separation instrument by an insured spouse on his or her life which is owned by the non-insured spouse, if the other requirements of Section 71 are met, will qualify as alimony or separate maintenance payments. Reg. Sec. 1.71-1T(b), Q/A-6. Such premium payments will be deductible under IRC Sec. 215. If the insured spouse owns the policy even though the non-insured spouse is the beneficiary, premium payments would not constitute alimony since they would not be payments "received by (or on behalf of) a spouse." IRC Section 71(b)(1)(A). Presumably, when an existing policy is transferred, the insured spouse may not deduct the cash surrender value as an alimony payment because it is not a cash payment. Reg. Sec. 1.71-1T(b), Q/A-5. If the insured spouse is required to continue the premium payments after the recipient spouse's death (e.g., where the children are the substitute beneficiaries), premium payments on such policies even during the life of the recipient spouse would not be alimony and deductible since the payments would not be required to end at the death of the recipient spouse. IRC Section 71(b)(1)(D).

In regard to pre-1985 divorce or separation instruments which have not been modified to expressly include the provisions of the new law, in order to be treated as alimony payments under the prior law, such payments had to be periodic and made in discharge of a legal obligation to support a former spouse arising out of a marital or family relationship.

Thus, under both pre-1985 and post-1984 law, the non-insured spouse must be the owner of the policy which is the subject of the premium payments. Rev. Rul. 70-218, 1970-1 C.B. 19. Reg. Sec. 1.71-1T(b), Q/A-6. Consequently, in determining what constitutes ownership by the non-insured spouse, the authorities under the pre-1985 law are instructive. If the insured spouse remains the owner of the insurance policy, the alimony deduction for premium payments will be denied even though the recipient spouse is the beneficiary and the owner spouse is prohibited from borrowing against the policy (Rev. Rul. 57-125, 1957-1 C.B. 27), the recipient spouse is designated irrevocable beneficiary (*Blumenthal v. Commissioner*, 183 F.2d 15 (3rd Cir. 1950)), or the recipient spouse is given the right to receive the cash surrender value of the policy (*Florence H. Griffith*, 35 T.C. 882). Even when the recipient spouse is the owner of the policy, premium payments by the insured spouse will not constitute alimony and be deductible if such ownership is subject to contingencies or substantial restrictions, such as the insured spouse's retention of the power to borrow against the policy, to withdraw its cash surrender value or to receive ownership of the policy in case of the death or remarriage of the recipient spouse. *Stevens v. Commissioner*, 439 F.2d 69 at 73 (2nd Cir. 1971). *Robert L. Montgomery, Jr.*, 13 T.C.M. 578 (1954).

Where a pre-1985 divorce or separation instrument was involved, the Tax Court and the Seventh Circuit have taken the position that premium payments for a term insurance policy do not constitute alimony and are not deductible by the non-insured spouse, on the theory that there is no economic benefit to the recipient spouse as would be the case with a whole life policy. *William H. Brodersen, Jr.*, 57 T.C. 412 (1971). *William C. Wright*, 62 T.C. 377 (1974), aff'm. 543 F.2d 593 (7th Cir. 1976). Although there is doubt whether the *Brodersen* and the *Wright* cases were a correct interpretation of the pre-1985 law, the new law clearly makes term as well as whole life premium payments eligible for alimony treatment. Reg. Sec. 1.71-1T, Q/A-6.

If the insurance policy is owned by an irrevocable trust (or some other third party) for the benefit of the recipient spouse, premium payments on such policy by the insured spouse will not constitute alimony and be deductible, since they are not received by the recipient spouse whose economic benefit is contingent upon the restrictions contained in the trust agreement. *Seligmann v. Commissioner*, 207 F.2d 489 (7th Cir. 1953). *Joseph N. Kinney, Jr.*, 17 T.C.M. 1039 (1958).

e. <u>Deductions and Welfare Benefit Funds</u>. If life insurance premiums are paid through a welfare benefit fund established by the employer, the contributions to the extent deductible under other provisions of the Code must meet additional restrictions on deductions under IRC Sections 419 and 419A. A detailed analysis of these provisions is beyond the scope of this paper. Generally, a fund includes a tax-exempt organization like a VEBA, any non-exempt trust, corporation or other organization and any accounts (e.g., reserves held by insurance companies) held for the employer by any person.

The amount deductible by the employer is limited to the "qualified direct cost" and any addition to a "qualified asset account" for the taxable year reduced by the fund's after-tax income (including employee contributions) during the taxable year. A "qualified direct cost" is the amount (including administration expenses) which would have been deductible had the employer been on a cash basis and provided the benefits directly, e.g., premiums paid for group insurance on the lives of active or retired employees. The "qualified asset account" consists of assets set aside for the payment of life insurance claims incurred but unpaid as of the close of the taxable year and the administrative cost with respect to such claims.

Special reserves under the qualified asset account can be set aside for post-retirement life insurance benefits but they must meet special nondiscrimination rules under IRC Section 505(b) and the reserve is limited to $50,000 (or a higher grandfathered amount) of group term insurance for a retiree. If the post-retirement life insurance benefit is for a key employee, there must be a separate account for each covered key employee and benefits must be paid only from that account. Key employee has the same meaning as the definition in IRC Section 416(i).

These new deduction limitations do not apply to plans involving ten or more employers if no employer normally contributes more than 10% of the total contributions under the plan by all employers. Furthermore, collective bargaining and employee pay-all plans are exempt from the statute. If an insurance carrier holds amounts under a qualified non-guaranteed contract, the amounts held under such contract will not be treated as a welfare benefit fund. A "qualified non-guaranteed contract" means any insurance contract (including a reasonable premium stablization reserve held thereunder) if there is no guarantee of a renewal of such contract and, other than insurance protection, the only payments to which the employer or employees are entitled are experience rated refunds or policy dividends which are not guaranteed and which are determined by factors other than the amount of welfare benefits paid to the employees of the employer or their beneficiaries.

6. Situations where premiums may be included in policyholder's income.

   a. Employee Compensation. If an employee owns the policy and the proceeds are payable to the employee's personal representative or estate or to any other beneficiary of such employee, the general rule is that the premiums paid on such a policy by the employer are taxable income to the insured employee. Reg. Sec. 1.61-2(d)(2)(ii)(a). If policy dividends are used to reduce premium payments, then only the net premiums paid by the employer are considered taxable income. See *Francis Weeks*, 16 T.C. 248 (1951). *Nelson H. Sturgis, Jr.*, 10 T.C.M. 136 (1951). What if the employer (not the employee) owns the policy but it is payable to a member of the employee's family? The above cited regulation suggests that the entire premium is taxable to the employee. However, the Tax Court rejected this argument by the government in a case where a corporate owned policy was payable to a trust for the benefit of the family of the insured president-shareholder where the corporation had the right to change the beneficiary. In *dicta*, the court suggested an amount equal to the one-year term life insurance protection might be includible in the income of the insured. *Ruth C. Rodebaugh*, 33 T.C.M. 169 (1974). Where the corporate owned policies were irrevocably payable to the wife and sons of the president-insured as beneficiaries, another court did include the entire premium payment by the corporation in the income of the insured. *Commissioner v. Bonwit*, 87 F.2d 764 (2nd Cir. 1937).

   In situations where the employer is the direct or indirect beneficiary of the insurance policy, there is no income to the employee. *Casale v. Commissioner*, 247 F.2d 440 (2nd Cir. 1957) (key person life insurance).

(1) Group Life Insurance. Special favorable tax rules apply to group term life insurance which meets the requirements of IRC Section 79 and IRC Section 89. (*See* item 12 for a more detailed discussion of group life insurance). As a general rule, the cost of such coverage is includible in the employee's gross income. However, the cost of group term life insurance coverage up to $50,000 is not taxable to the employee. IRC Section 79(a). A disabled former employee receives a total exclusion of group term insurance coverage. IRC Section 79(b)(1). For tax years beginning after 1983, the previous total exclusion of group term life insurance coverage from the income of a retired employee was changed to impose a $50,000 ceiling on the amount of such coverage. IRC Section 79(e). Under statutory grandfather provisions, the total exclusion of group term insurance coverage still applies to certain retired employees -- (i) an employee retired before 1984 and covered by a group insurance plan at the date of retirement and that plan (or a comparable successor) was in existence on January 1, 1984 or (ii) an employee who retires after 1983 if he was at least 55 years of age on or before January 1, 1984, was employed during 1983 and is covered by a group insurance plan which was in existence on January 1, 1984 or a comparable successor to such plan except for an employee who retires after 1986 and the plan discriminates in favor of key employees. Reg. Sec. 1.79-4T, Q/A-1.

In determining his or her overall insurance coverage, an employee must combine all group coverage and will be entitled to exclude from reported income only that expense incurred for the first $50,000 of the aggregate coverage. If the employee shares the cost of coverage with the employer, that portion paid by the employee will first be allocated to the coverage over the $50,000 amount. Reg. Sec. 1.79-3(e)(1).

The cost of the coverage over the $50,000 exempt amount is determined on a monthly basis as follows: (i) determine the total amount of group term life insurance coverage for the employee in each calendar month of his taxable year (if a change occurs during any month, take the average at the beginning and end of the month); (ii) subtract $50,000 from each month's coverage; (iii) to the balance, if any, for each month, apply the appropriate rate from Table I found in Reg. Sec. 1.79-3(d)(2) setting forth the cost of group-term life insurance coverage at various ages; and (iv) from the sum of the monthly cost, subtract the total employee contributions for the year.

Employer payment of premiums on group term insurance on the lives of dependents of an employee is not excluded from the employee's income under Section 79. Reg. Sec. 1.79-3(f)(2). However, a regulation under IRC Section 61 excludes from the employee's income the cost of such dependent group term coverage if it does not exceed $2,000. Reg. Sec. 1.61-2(d)(2)(ii)(b). Some doubt has been thrown upon the continuing validity of the exclusionary provisions of such regulation by a recent amendment to IRC Section 61 which expressly includes in the definition of gross income compensation from fringe benefits.

Under certain circumstances, a group term life insurance policy may provide for a permanent benefit but the cost of the permanent benefit reduced by the amount paid for the permanent benefit by the employee is included in the employee's income. Reg. Sec. 1.79-1(b) and (d).

(2) <u>Insurance in a Qualified Plan</u>. If a life insurance contract is purchased by a IRC Section 403(a) plan or by a trust described in IRC Section 401(a) which is exempt from tax under IRC Section 501(a), the cost of the protection to the employee is includible in his gross income for the taxable year if the proceeds of the contract are payable directly or indirectly to the employee or his beneficiary. IRC Section 72(m)(3). (For a more detailed discussion of life insurance in qualified benefit plans see item 13). This includes insurance protection payable to the trustee of the plan if under the terms of the plan the trustee is required to pay over all of the proceeds to the employee's beneficiary. Reg. Sec. 1.72-16(b)(1). Conversely, the employee is not taxed on the cost of any insurance protection where the

proceeds are payable to the trustee if the trust has a right under any circumstances to retain any part of the proceeds. Reg. Sec. 1.72-16(b)(6). *See* Rev. Rul. 66-138, 1966-1 C.B. 25. The cost of insurance protection on the life of some person in whom the employee has an insurable interest will also be included in the gross income of the employee. P.L.R. 8426090. The cost of current life insurance protection from a policy in a qualified pension or profit sharing plan is includible in the employee's gross income even though the plan contains certain forfeiture provisions applicable only to the cash surrender value of the policy. *Ross H. Funkhouser,* 58 T.C. 940 (1972).

In regard to whole life insurance policies, the current life insurance protection for the employee is the amount of policy coverage in excess of the cash value of the policy at the end of the taxable year. Reg. Sec. 1.71-16(b)(3). The cost is determined in connection with a one-year term rate table (the "P.S. 58 cost table") in Rev. Rul. 55-747, 1955-2 C.B. 228 as amplified by Rev. Rul. 66-110, 1966-C.B. 12. The 1966 ruling allows the employee to measure the current insurance protection cost by reference to the one-year term table for initial issue standard risks maintained by the insurance carrier issuing the whole life insurance policy, if the rates contained in such table are lower than those contained in the P.S. 58 cost table. Note that the carrier's term table must be for initial issue insurance for standard risks. Accordingly, the premium tables for dividend option term insurance and the preferred rates offered to non-smoking persons cannot be used. Rev. Rul. 67-154, 1967-1 C.B. 11. P.L.R. 8547006.

Presumably, if the qualified benefit plan owns a term insurance policy on the life of the employee, the entire cost of the current insurance protection is also measured by the above cited revenue rulings, although some contend that the cost is equal to the actual premium paid on that policy.

If there are nondeductible employee contributions to the plan, any insurance premiums paid by the plan are presumed to be paid first from the employer contributions before use of the employee contributions unless the plan expressly provides otherwise. Rev. Rul. 68-390, 1968-2 C.B. 175. Of course, to the extent that nondeductible employee contributions are used to pay premiums, the cost of current insurance protection attributable to such premiums would not be current income to the employee. The cost of current insurance protection is included in the employee's gross income in the year that the premium is paid by the plan, without apportionment, even though the policy year overlaps the employee's tax year. IRC Sec. 72(m)(3)(B).

(3) Split Dollar Life Insurance. Under a traditional split dollar life insurance arrangement, the employee must report as income the economic value of the benefit received from participation in the plan. Rev. Rul. 64-328, 1964-2 C.B. 11. (*See* item 10 for a more detailed discussion of split dollar life insurance). The benefit received by the employee is considered to be the current insurance coverage provided by the split dollar arrangement. The value of this coverage is calculated using the government's P.S. 58 cost table rates for one-year term premiums. See Rev. Rul. 55-747, *supra*, as amplified by Rev. Rul. 66-110, *supra*. If the rates for such coverage issued by the insurance company are lower than those contained in the P.S. 58 cost table, the lower rates may be used to determine the amount of taxable income reported by the employee. Rev. Rul. 66-110, *supra*. However, preferred rates cannot be used (P.L.R. 8547006) nor dividend option rates (Rev. Rul. 67-154, *supra*). In addition, any policy dividends benefiting the employee and any employee ownership of policy cash value attributable to employer contributions are also includible in the employee's gross income. Rev. Rul. 66-110, *supra*. P.L.R. 7916029. P.L.R. 8310027.

b. Shareholder Dividends. Premium payments are considered taxable income (i.e., a distribution of dividends) to the shareholder if the corporation pays the premiums on policies owned by the shareholder and such policies are used by the shareholder for personal purposes. *Thomas E. Brock, Jr.*, 44 T.C.M. 128 (1982). One case has suggested that there may be P.S. 58 cost dividend income to a shareholder for a corporate-owned policy payable to the shareholder's beneficiary where the corporation reserved the right to change the beneficiary. *Ruth C. Rodebaugh, supra.* In Rev. Rul. 79-50, 1979-1 C.B. 138, a split dollar plan between a corporation and an insured non-employee stockholder was determined to have provided a benefit taxable to the stockholder as a distribution in the form of dividends.

There is no dividend income to a stockholder for premiums paid by a corporation on an insurance policy designed to fund a stock redemption agreement between the stockholder and the corporation regardless of whether the corporation is the owner of the policy, the stockholder has the right to designate a beneficiary or the proceeds are payable to the stockholder or a trustee. *Prunier v. Commissioner*, 248 F.2d 818 (1st Cir. 1957). Rev. Rul. 59-184, 1959-1 C.B. 65. However, if a corporation pays the premiums on insurance policies owned by stockholders to finance a cross-purchase agreement among the stockholders, such payments will be considered dividends to the various shareholders who are the owners and beneficiaries of the policies. Rev. Rul. 59-184, *supra* at 67. However, the amount of income to the shareholder can be greatly reduced if the corporation pays the premiums pursuant to a split dollar arrangement.

c. <u>Alimony Premium Payments</u>. Generally, premium payments that are paid pursuant to a divorce or separation instrument executed after 1984 will qualify as taxable alimony to the non-insured spouse provided that the non-insured spouse if the owner of the policy. Temp. Reg. Sec. 1.71-1T, Q/A-6. Basically, the same rule applies to premium payments made pursuant to divorce or separation instruments executed before 1985 if the non-insured spouse is the owner of the policy with no reversion rights in favor of the insured spouse. Since the same rules apply to the deductibility of alimony payments under IRC Section 215 as apply to the income inclusion of such payments under IRC Section 71, see the more detailed discussion under deduction of alimony premium payments in item 5.

7. Policy Loan Interest Deductibility.

a. Personal Policy Loan Interest. Since January 1, 1987, within limits imposed by the Internal Revenue Code, investment interest, trade or business interest and passive activity interest remain deductible. Subject to a phase-out ending in 1991, personal interest is not deductible except for interest on a debt which is secured by the taxpayer's principal or second residence and interest incurred on the extended payment of estate taxes. IRC Section 163(h). An insurance policy purchased outside of a trade or business context is not considered an investment and the interest incurred on a loan to pay the premiums on such policy would be personal interest. General Explanation of Tax Reform Act of 1986, p. 266 ("Blue Book TRA 86"). The personal interest deduction for loans to pay premiums on an insurance policy is subject to a phase-in disallowance equal to 35% in 1987, 60% in 1988, 80% in 1989, 90% in 1990 and 100% in 1991 and later. IRC Section 163(h)(6).

b. Policy Loans as Investment Interest or Passive Activity Interest. Interest incurred on a loan will be classified as personal, trade or business, investment, or passive activity by tracing the disbursements of the loan to specific expenditures. Reg. Sec. 1.163-8T(a)(3). Presumably, if money is borrowed against the cash value of a policy or an individually owned policy is pledged for a loan and the proceeds are used for an investment or passive activity expenditure, such interest would be investment interest or passive activity interest deductible subject to limitations in the Code. However, there is some question as to whether, despite a direct link between a policy loan and an investment or passive activity expenditure, the IRS might still treat the loan as being for the purpose of personal premium payments rather than for investments. Although involving a single premium policy, the Service has taken the position that a direct loan against the policy or the pledging of the policy as collateral for a loan had the main purpose of carrying the policy despite the fact that the loan proceeds were used to purchase stock. Rev. Rul. 79-41, 1979-1 C.B. 124. G.C.M. 39534. Although a single premium policy has its own peculiar nondeductibility rules under IRC Section 264, such a position by the Service of the main purpose of the loan might be inferred to apply to policies that are not single premium in nature.

c. Policy Loan Limitations For Trade and Business Interest. With regard to policies purchased after June 20, 1986, only the interest on the first $50,000 of policy loans is deductible. For those policies purchased before June 21, 1986, there is no limit. In effect, no deduction is allowed for interest on aggregate borrowing exceeding $50,000 against post-June 20, 1986 policies covering the life of any one officer or employee of the policy owner or any other person financially interested in any trade or business carried on by the policy owner. IRC Section 264(a)(4). Regardless of the use to which the loan proceeds are put, the deduction is disallowed for the interest on the indebtedness that exceeds $50,000 per individual.

(1) Which Contracts Are Grandfathered - Purchased After June 20, 1986? If the policy was applied for before June 21, 1986, in most instances the policy is grandfathered, though it is actually issued after June 20, 1986. Blue Book TRA 86, p. 580. The date of application governs even if the insurance carrier's bid is conditioned upon a determination that the person to be insured is an insurable risk. 132 Cong. Rec. S8290 (Sen. Dole, June 24, 1986). Thus a policy applied for and issued after June 20, 1986, but backdated for age purposes would not be grandfathered.

(2) What Can Cause A Grandfathered Policy To Lose That Status? If a grandfathered policy is sold, exchanged, transferred or modified after June 20, 1986, the question arises as to whether it will be considered a new policy not benefiting from the grandfathering rules. The exchange of a grandfathered policy for a new policy issued by the same insurer does not trigger the new interest deduction ceiling. However, an exchange for a policy issued by a different insurer would. If there are minor administrative changes in a grandfathered policy such as changes in the address of the insurer, the officers of the insurer, or the address of the insured, such changes will not lose grandfathered status. Blue Book TRA 86, p. 580. Senators Dole and Packwood have stated on the floor of the Senate that the following

additional modifications to a grandfathered policy are acceptable: change in the owner of the policy, change in loan rates, exercise of an option or a right granted under the contract as originally issued such as the substitution of an insured but excluding conversion to term insurance and any other change that was contemplated by the parties and is customary with respect to such insurance. 132 Cong. Rec. S13956 (September 27, 1986). However, Congressman Rostenkowski has gone on record that the House does not necessarily agree with the statements by Senators Dole and Packwood and particularly expressed reservations about the statements concerning the contractual ability to substitute insureds. 132 Cong. Rec. E3391 (October 2, 1986). Until further clarification comes from the IRS, except for exchange of contracts involving the same insurance company and the minor administrative changes mentioned in the Blue Book TRA 86, the safe approach is not to change the owners or insureds or to exercise any significant policy options for a grandfathered trade or business policy. If any such action must be taken, then the action probably should stay within the parameters of the statements by Senators Dole and Packwood.

(3) Separate Businesses Are Aggregated. If a taxpayer carries on more than one trade or business, the $50,000 amount per officer, employee or other person financially interested in the trade or business of the taxpayer is determined on an aggregate basis for each such person in all trades or businesses of the taxpayer. A controlled group of corporations is treated as one taxpayer and unincorporated trades or businesses with common ownership are treated as one taxpayer. Blue Book TRA 86, p. 579.

(4) Borrowing Against or Pledging Policy for Business Purposes. The $50,000 ceiling does apply to insurance contract loans even though the proceeds are used in a trade or business. Blue Book TRA 86, p. 580. Senators Dole and Packwood have stated that the $50,000 ceiling does not apply to interest on third party business loans secured by the pledge of an insurance policy. 132 Cong. Rec. S13957

(September 27, 1986). The Conference Report and the Blue Book are silent on the policy pledge question. The difference in interest deduction treatment between direct business loans against the policy and pledging a policy to secure a third party loan could be justified by the fact that, unlike most commercial loans, the employer is not obligated to repay a policy loan which may remain outstanding until the employee's death. *See* 132 Cong. Rec. S8052 (Sen. Dole, June 20, 1986). Until the IRS clarifies its position on this issue, the deductibility of interest on a trade or business loan in excess of $50,000 secured by a policy on the life of an officer, employee or a person financially interested in the trade or business is questionable.

d. <u>Additional Limitations Imposed on Single Premium Contracts</u>. IRC Section 264(a)(2) denies the deduction of interest paid or accrued on indebtedness incurred to purchase or continue in effect a single premium life insurance contract purchased after March 1, 1954. For purposes of Section 264, a single premium life insurance contract is defined as a policy on which substantially all the premiums on the contract are paid within a four year period from the date of purchase, or a policy on which an amount is deposited after March 1, 1954, with the insurer for payment of a substantial number of future premiums. IRC Section 264(b). Although the statute and regulations do not define what Congress meant by "substantially all" and "substantial number", there has been some judicial guidance in this area. The Tax Court has held that prepayment of 75% of the premium within the first four years was not "substantially all" of the premiums on the contract. *Frederick A. Dudderar*, 44 T.C. 632 (1965), acq. 1966-2 C.B. 4. Whether a substantial number of premiums have been prepaid depends upon the relationship of the number of future payments to the number of payments which normally would be required to keep the insurance contract in effect which could be based upon the life expectancy of the insured. One court found that the prepayment of 5 out of 20 premiums was not a substantial number. *Goldman v. United States*, 403 F.2d 776 (10th Cir. 1968). Another case found that a substantial number was not involved for four different policies when the prepayment of four premiums was compared to the estimated premium payments of 38, 34, 32 and 14 for the respective policies. *Campbell v. Cen-Tex, Inc.* 377 F.2d 688 (5th Cir. 1967). Pledging or borrowing against an already existing single premium policy can still be treated as an indebtedness incurred to carry a single premium policy with the consequence disallowance of the deduction of interest on the loan secured by the pledge of or the loan against the policy. *See* Rev. Rul. 79-41, 1979-1 C.B. 124 and G.C.M. 39534 involving an annuity contract.

There are questions concerning the applicability of the single premium interest prohibition of Section 264(a)(2) to flexible premium contracts. Technically, no premiums are ever due on a universal life policy as long as there is sufficient cash value to pay the monthly mortality and expense charges. Thus, could payments under a universal life policy be considered a series of single premium contracts? Fortunately, the Conference Committee Report and the Blue Book state that "no inference is intended that universal life insurance policies are always treated as single premium contracts." Blue Book TRA 86, p. 580. However, even if all universal life policies are not automatically single premium, if the insured deposits a large amount of cash into the universal life policy at any time (not just for the first four years) delaying the need for future premium payments for many years, it may very well be treated as a single premium policy. Thus, to minimize the single premium argument, the policy owner should pay a significant premium on the universal life policy each year and avoid placing a large amount of cash into the policy in any one year which would eliminate the need for future premium payments for many years. If a large cash value in an existing policy is to be used to purchase a new universal life policy, the transfer of the cash should be accomplished through a tax-free exchange under IRC Section 1035.

e. Additional Limitations Imposed Upon Financing Continuing Premium Payments. Any amount paid or accrued on indebtedness incurred or continued to purchase or carry a life insurance contract (other than single premium) pursuant to a plan of purchase which contemplates the systematic direct or indirect borrowing of part or all of the increases in the cash value of the contract (from the insurer or otherwise) will be disallowed as a deduction unless one of four exceptions discussed below apply. This applies only with respect to contracts purchased after August 6, 1963. IRC Section 264(a)(3).

(1) Pursuant to a Plan of Purchase. Whether the borrowing is in connection with a plan of purchase of insurance is a fact question to be determined after reviewing all of the circumstances. The plan need not be in existence at the date the policy is purchased but may come into existence at a later date up to seven years after the policy is issued (or after a substantial increase in premiums). There is a rebuttable presumption of the existence of a plan if three or more premiums are borrowed. Reg. Sec. 1.264-4(c)(1)(i).

(2) Direct or Indirect Borrowing of Cash Value Increase. The statutory prohibition covers interest on loans, not only from the insurance carrier, but also from a bank or any other person. A third party loan need not involve a pledge of the insurance contract but may contemplate unsecured borrowing or the use of other property. Reg. Sec. 1.264-4(c)(2). Rev. Rul. 74-500, 1974-2 C.B. 91.

(3) Grandfathered Contracts. As noted earlier, the prohibition for deduction of interest on indebtedness incurred or continued to purchase or carry a life insurance contract pursuant to a plan of systematic borrowing of cash value applies only to contracts purchased after August 6, 1963. A grandfathered contract purchased or acquired whether from the insurer, insured or any other person after August 6, 1963 will lose its grandfathered status. Policies transferred by gift, bequest, inheritance or in a transaction to which IRC Section 381(a) applies of a contract issued before August 7, 1963 will remain exempt from the statutory prohibition. Reg. Sec. 1.264-4(e). If a grandfathered contract is exchanged for another contract, the new contract is subject to the interest deductibility limitations even though the exchange was tax-free under IRC Section 1035. P.L.R. 8816015.

(4) Exceptions. There are four exceptions to the general rule that the deduction of interest will be disallowed on an indebtedness incurred or

continued to purchase or carry a life insurance policy pursuant to a plan of systematic borrowing of the increases in cash value: the 4 out of 7 exception, the $100 a year exception, the unforeseen events exception, and the trade or business exception. Reg. Sec. 1.264-4(d). Thus, even if there is a plan of systematic borrowing, the exceptions avoid the statutory prohibition of interest deductions.

(a) The 4 out of 7 Exception. If no part of four of the annual premiums due during the first seven years after the issuance date of the policy is paid under a plan by means of indebtedness, interest on indebtedness with respect to such policy will be deductible for the life of the policy. In determining whether all or part of a year's premium has been paid by means of indebtedness, the aggregate premiums on such policy during the policy year (rather than the taxpayer's year) will be used. Reg. Sec. 1.264-4(d)(1)(i). Thus, if any part of a premium is paid by borrowing, the entire policy year is tainted for the 4 out of 7 exception. If the indebtedness with respect to the policy during any one policy year exceeds the annual premium, then the excess borrowing will be allocated to the prior policy years beginning with the most recent. If the indebtedness exceeds the aggregate premiums for the current and all prior policy years, the excess indebtedness will be applied to future policy years if there has been a prepayment of premiums. Reg. Sec. 1.264-4(d)(1)(ii). Thus, a loan against the cash value of a policy in excess of the current year's premium will taint not only the current policy year but one or more of the prior policy years in applying the exception.

    Once more than three premiums have been borrowed during the first seven years, the exception is not applicable even though the policy owner might repay the loans before the end of the seven year period. Rev. Rul. 72-609, 1972-2 C.B. 199.

Within the first seven years, if a policy is transferred for valuable consideration or gratuitously, a new seven year period does not start with the transfer and the subsequent owners of the policy can tack on the years of ownership by the previous owners in applying the 4 out of 7 exception. Rev. Rul. 71-309, 1971-2 C.B. 168. This also means that any years tainted by a prior owner's indebtedness will also be counted in the application of the 4 out of 7 exception to the new owner. However, if a grandfathered policy issued on or before August 6, 1963 is the subject of a tax-free exchange for a new insurance policy, the new policy must be requalified under the 4 out of 7 exception since this would be a purchase for value after August 6, 1963. P.L.R. 8816015.

Since Reg. Sec. 1.264-4(d)(1) only applies to indebtedness created during the first seven years, presumably, once the 4 out of 7 rule is met during the first seven years, there are no limits upon the amount of indebtedness and deductibility of interest (subject to other provisions of the Code) and the policy owner thereafter could borrow the entire cash value, including the accumulations during the first seven years. However, the regulations provide that if there is a substantial increase in any annual premium on the contract, a new seven year period begins on the date such increased premium is paid. Reg. Sec. 1.264-4(d)(1)(i). There are no authorities concerning what constitutes a "substantial increase" in premiums.

As noted earlier, technically, no premiums are ever due on a universal life insurance policy. Thus, a question has been raised whether a universal life policy can ever qualify under the 4 out of 7 exception. Assuming that the 4 out of 7 exception is applicable to a universal life policy, the flexibility of premium payments raises the additional question as to whether a new seven year period begins every time there is a substantial increase in a premium payment. This question can be avoided by making premium payments that are substantially the same from year to year, but what is the result should a particular premium be missed because of cash flow problems of the policy owner? Again assuming that a universal life contract can qualify under the 4 out of 7 exception and premium payments vary during the first seven years of the policy, what is the premium measure for determining how much the policy-owner may borrow against the policy during the first seven years without tainting more than three years? Presumably, the premium measure would be the lowest annual premium during the first seven years (which could be zero) which would mean that the largest amount that could be borrowed against the policy would be three times that lowest premium amount. *See* Reg. Sec. 1.264-4(c)(1)(ii).

(b) The $100 Exception. If the interest incurred does not exceed $100 for the taxable year of the taxpayer, the interest deduction will be allowed regardless of whether there is a systematic plan of borrowing. For this purpose, all of the policies subject to all of the plans of systematic borrowing will be aggregated together. However, if such interest incurred exceeds $100, the entire amount of interest incurred is nondeductible. Reg. Sec. 1.264-4(d)(2).

(c) Unforeseen Events Exception. If there is an unforeseen substantial loss of income or an unforeseen substantial increase in financial liability which results in the taxpayer incurring the debt to carry the policy, the deduction will be allowed even though the loan is directly used to pay premiums. Thus, the plan of systematic borrowing must arise because of the unforeseen event. If at the time the policy was purchased the event of financial stress could have been foreseen, such as college education expenses (except to the extent that substantial increases of such expenses were not foreseen), the interest deduction will be disallowed. Reg. Sec. 1.264-4(d)(3).

(d) Trade or Business Exception. The interest deduction will be allowed if the indebtedness is incurred in connection with the taxpayer's trade or business. Therefore, the interest deductions will be allowed if the taxpayer can prove that the amounts borrowed against the policy were actually used for business purposes. However, if the taxpayer borrows to finance certain business life insurance (such as key man, split dollar, or stock retirement plans), such loans are not considered to have been incurred in connection with the taxpayer's trade or business. Reg. Sec. 1.264-4(d)(4). *American Body & Equipment Co. v. United States*, 511 F.2d 647 (5th Cir. 1975). Likewise, the trade or business exception does not apply to systematic borrowing against the cash value of an insurance policy to fund an employee retirement plan. Rev. Rul. 81-255, 1981-2 C.B. 79. Whether funds borrowed are used for trade or business or to finance cash value business life insurance is a question of fact and circumstances. Interest on loans to carry on a business will not be disallowed merely because funds which could have been used to reduce those loans is used to purchase key man insurance. However, if the amount of other business loans increase each year by an amount equal to the premium payments on a key person policy, the interest deduction might be disallowed. Reg. Sec. 1.264-4(d)(4), Exs. (1) and (2).

f. Defective Trusts. If the trustee of an unfunded irrevocable insurance trust borrows against the policy held in the trust and if the grantor is treated as the owner of the trust, the grantor is allowed to take a deduction for any interest incurred to the same extent as any other owner of the policy. IRC Section 671. Trusts which are treated as being owned by the grantor are sometimes called "defective trusts" because the pass through of income and expense deductions is generally considered undesirable. However, if the desired income tax deduction from a trust which produces no income can be passed through to the grantor, the use of these types of trusts are generally considered prudent tax planning. However, the usefulness of the interest pass through of a defective life insurance trust is being decreased since the deduction for personal interest is being phased out over a five year period beginning in 1987. IRC Section 163(h)(6).

Not all of the grantor trust rules of IRC Section 671-677 are appropriate for creating a defective life insurance trust since many of the rules would include the insurance policy and its proceeds in the grantor's gross estate for federal estate tax purposes such as a reversionary interest in excess of 5% and the power to revoke. However, there are several defects under the grantor trust rule which might obtain the desired tax deduction without estate tax inclusion.

(1) Defects Under IRC Section 674(c). No grantor is treated as the owner of a trust in which the powers held by and solely exercisable by an independent trustee (none of whom is the grantor and no more than half of whom are related or subordinate parties) includes the right to distribute trust income or principal to a class of beneficiaries. However, this safe harbor from the application of the grantor trust rules does not apply if the trustee can add to the class of beneficiaries except for after-born or after-adopted children. IRC Section 674(c). Therefore, to create a defective trust under Section 674(c), one possible alternative used by some practitioners would be to provide the independent trustee with the power to name an additional beneficiary (e.g., a charity) of the trust property although there are no authorities which have considered the income and estate tax implications of the creation of a defective trust in this manner.

(2) Defects Under IRC Section 675(4)(C). The grantor is to be treated as the owner of a trust if the power to reacquire trust principal by substituting other property of an equivalent value is exercisable by any one person in a nonfiduciary capacity without the express approval or consent of the then-serving trust

fiduciary. IRC Section 675(4)(C). Therefore, the grantor may want to retain the power to reacquire insurance policies transferred to the trust in exchange for other insurance policies of equivalent value in order to create a defective trust under this Section. The Tax Court has held that such a power retained by a grantor caused no estate tax problems under IRC Section 2038 (revocable transfers) or Section 2042 (incidents of ownership). *Estate of Jordahl*, 65 T.C. 92 (1975), acq. 1977-1 C.B. 1. Since the trust involved in that case pre-dated the applicability of IRC Section 2036 (retained life estate), no decision was rendered as to the applicability of that estate tax section.

(3) Defects Under IRC Section 677(a)(1)-(2). Another often used defect is to authorize the trustee (who is not an adverse party) to distribute or to accumulate for future distribution to the grantor's spouse trust income. The IRS has allowed the pass through of the interest deduction from the trust to the grantor under this grantor trust provision. P.L.R. 7909031. P.L.R. 8008085. This defect will no longer work if the marriage should terminate because of the death or divorce of the grantor's spouse. In order to prevent inclusion of the trust property in the grantor's gross estate, the trustee should be prohibited from using trust income to discharge the grantor's legal obligations to support the grantor's spouse. Also, the new anti-freeze provisions of IRC Section 2036(c) might have an impact upon the includability in the gross estate of the insured grantor of an insurance policy included in an irrevocable life insurance trust of which the insured's spouse is a beneficiary.

(4) Defects Under IRC Section 677(a)(3). The defect most commonly used is to authorize the trustee (who is not an adverse party) to use trust income to pay premiums on the insurance policy on the life of the grantor or the grantor's spouse. Even though there was no income contemplated from the life insurance trust, the IRS has allowed the pass through of interest deduction from the trust to the grantor under this Section in several private letter rulings.

P.L.R. 8007080. P.L.R. 8014078. P.L.R. 8103074. P.L.R. 8112087. P.L.R. 8118051. P.L.R. 8126047. The Tax Court has held that the use of trust income to pay insurance premiums on the grantor's life is not a retained life interest under the predecessor of IRC Section 2036(a)(1). *First National Bank of Birmingham*, 36 B.T.A. 651 (1937), acq. 1937-2 C.B. 24. *See* also, Rev. Rul. 81-164, 1981-1 C.B. 458. However, note that the trust in this case possessed income-producing assets in addition to the insurance policies.

(5) IRS Ruling Moratorium. Despite the favorable private letter rulings cited above, the IRS announced on August 24, 1981, that it is studying the subject of the pass through of income, deductions and credits for defective trusts. In addition, the IRS will no longer issue private letter rulings on such issues until it has announced its position officially. Rev. Proc. 88-3, Sec. 5.23, 1988-1 I.R.B. 29 at 35. This restriction on new issuances of private letter rulings will apply to a trust when (1) the trust corpus consists or will consist substantially of insurance policies on the life of the grantor or the grantor's spouse, (2) the trustee or any other person has a power to apply the trust's income or corpus to the payment of premiums on policies of insurance on the life of the grantor or the grantor's spouse, (3) the trustee or any other person has the power to use the trust's assets to make loans to the grantor's estate or to purchase assets from the grantor's estate, and (4) there is a right or power in any person that would cause the grantor to be treated as the owner of all or a portion of the trust under Sections 673 to 677.

g. Timing of Interest Deduction. Although an accrual basis taxpayer may deduct otherwise deductible interest expenses in the years such interest accrues without payment, a cash basis taxpayer can only deduct the interest in the year that the interest has been paid. IRC Section 163(a). For a cash basis taxpayer, interest is not deemed to be paid if unpaid interest on an existing policy loan is treated as an additional policy loan and added to the principal. Rev. Rul. 73-482, 1973-2 C.B. 44. A cash basis taxpayer cannot deduct interest owing to an insurance company which is deducted by the company from the proceeds of a new loan with the balance remitted to the taxpayer. *Keith v. Commissioner*, 139 F.2d 596 (2nd Cir. 1944). However, the taxpayer may deduct the interest which has been added to the principal of the policy loan in a later year when it is actually paid. *Estell Cheeseman*, 28 T.C.M. 1334 (1969). Upon the death of the insured, any unpaid interest added to the principal of loans against insurance policies is deemed to be paid at the time the insurance carrier reduces the death benefit by the amount of the loan and accrued interest. *Estate of Pat E. Hooks*, 22 T.C. 502 (1954), acq. 1955-1 C.B. 5.

A person cannot deduct the payment of interest on a policy loan against an insurance policy owned by someone else, *J. Simpson Dean*, 35 T.C. 1083 (1963), nor can the assignee of an insurance policy deduct interest accrued on a policy loan before the date of assignment, *Agnes I. Fox*, 43 B.T.A. 895 (1941). When payments are made to reduce a policy loan consisting of past due premium and interest payments, it is presumed that the payments are used first to reduce the premium loan before the interest loan. *Hiram W. Evans*, 5 T.C.M. 346 (1946). However, if the insurance carrier treats a portion of the loan payment as a reduction of the interest loan, that portion of the payment will be deductible. *Murray Kay*, 44 T.C. 660 (1965).

Although it is clear that a cash basis taxpayer may not deduct the interest on a policy loan which is not directly paid but merely added to the principal of the existing loan, questions may arise where the interest is paid with the proceeds from a second loan from some third party or where the interest is paid directly to the insurance carrier but an additional loan in the amount of the interest payment is taken against the policy shortly before or shortly after the interest payment. Although there are no authorities considering such situations involving the payment of interest on a life insurance policy loan, there are authorities considering similar situations involving other types of loans. Clearly, if interest is paid to one lender by a cash basis taxpayer with funds borrowed from a second lender, the interest is deductible when paid. *Franklin v. Commissioner*, 683 F.2d 125 (5th Cir. 1982). However, courts have not always agreed as to the deductibility of interest when paid with proceeds from a second loan received from the original lender. The Tax Court has allowed such a deduction when the second loan was not solely for the purpose of paying interest, the proceeds of the second loan were commingled with other funds so as to lose their identity, the creditor possessed sufficient other funds to have made the interest payment and the lender lost control of the second loan. *Newton Burgess*, 8 T.C. 47 (1947). Other cases have noted the existence of criticism of the *Burgess* test and have denied deductibility of interest when there was an exchange of checks in identical amounts representing the receipt of the proceeds of the second loan and the payment of interest on the first loan or where the taxpayer specifically earmarked a portion of the second loan proceeds for the purpose of paying interest due. *Battelstein v. Commissioner*, 631 F.2d 1182 (5th Cir. 1980). *Wilkerson v. Commissioner*, 655 F.2d 980 (9th Cir. 1981). Thus, the *Burgess* tests put emphasis upon the unrestricted control of the second loan proceeds by the taxpayer while *Battelstein* and *Wilkerson* emphasized the purpose of the second loan. *Norman W. Menz*, 80 T.C. 1174 (1983). The IRS has stated in a technical advice memorandum that it will follow the four *Burgess* tests, but not in the situation where the payment of interest with borrowed funds is a prearranged step transaction in which the debtor and creditor merely exchanged checks to create an interest deduction for the debtor. T.A.M. 8415002.

Thus, if the interest on a life insurance policy loan is paid with the proceeds from a loan from a different creditor, the interest will be deductible. If the interest on a life insurance policy loan is paid by the policyholder and he receives proceeds from an additional policy loan either shortly before or shortly after the interest payment, the interest may or may not be deductible under the above tests, depending upon the particular fact situation.

8. Life Insurance and Corporate Alternative Minimum Tax.

Corporations frequently own life insurance policies in connection with buy-sell agreements, key person insurance, salary continuation plans and other employee benefits. Unfortunately, TRA 86 put a damper on the attractiveness of corporate owned life insurance by the corporate alternative minimum tax provisions promulgated under IRC Sections 55 through 59.

The alternative minimum tax imposed on corporations is equal to 20 percent or the alternative minimum taxable income base of the corporation. IRC Section 55(b). Alternative minimum taxable income is determined by adding a list of tax preference items and making some adjustments to the regular taxable income of the corporation. The corporation will have to pay this tax if it exceeds the corporation's regular taxable income liability for its taxable year. IRC Section 55(a).

a. Book Income and Adjusted Current Earnings Adjustment. Among the adjustments to the alternative minimum taxable income calculation is a book income adjustment providing for an increase in the regular taxable income base by an amount equal to 50 percent of the book income over alternative minimum taxable income (including all preferences except this book income adjustment and the alternative tax net operating loss deduction). IRC Section 56(c)(1). The book income adjustment applies for taxable years beginning in 1987, 1988 and 1989. IRC Section 56(f)(1). For tax years beginning after 1989, the corporation's alternative minimum taxable income is to be adjusted by the adjusted current earnings adjustment. IRC Section 56(g)(1).

   The book income adjustment is based on adjusted net book income which is the income reported by the corporation on an applicable financial statement, after certain adjustments. IRC Section 56(f)(2).

b. Impact on Life Insurance. Book income is affected by corporate owned life insurance. Corporate owned life insurance will increase book income by the excess of the annual increase in cash surrender value over the annual premium for the policy. Book income will decrease by the excess of the annual premium over the annual increase in cash surrender value. Book income will increase by the amount of death proceeds over the policy's cash surrender value.

   Fifty percent of the amount by which the corporation's adjusted net book income exceeds its alternative minimum taxable income must be added to its alternative minimum taxable income. Therefore, up to 50 percent of the cash value buildup or proceeds realized by a corporation might be added to its alternative minimum taxable income base. Such amounts might be subject to the 20 percent alternative minimum tax.

Beginning for taxable years after 1989, the alternative minimum taxable income of corporations shall be increased by 75 percent of the excess (if any) of the adjusted current earnings (similar to earnings and profits) of the corporation over alternative minimum taxable income. IRC Section 56 (g). This adjustment replaces the book income adjustment and similarly provides for the inclusion of the elements of life insurance contracts. IRC Section 56(g)(B)(ii).

To the extent it exceeds the normal tax liability, the new alternative minimum tax provisions can impose a substantial alternative minimum tax liability on corporations owning life insurance policies. The additional tax liability can substantially reduce the funds available to the corporation. If the life insurance proceeds were intended to provide funds for redemption agreements, to meet contractual obligations to survivors of a deceased employee, or to compensate the corporation for the loss of a key employee, a shortfall in the funding may result because of possible alternative minimum tax liability.

The possibility of alternative minimum tax liability must, therefore, be considered by all corporate policyholders. However, it is difficult to isolate specific techniques to deal with the potential taxation of a life insurance policy because it is impossible to accurately predict whether or not there will be a tax and to what extent and when the tax will occur.

c. Steps to Avoid. There are several ways to avoid the tax. One way if S Corporation status, because the alternative minimum tax is not applicable to S Corporations, since Subchapter S income is taxed at the individual shareholder level. The individual alternative minimum tax applies to taxable income, which neither includes life insurance cash values nor proceeds. Another is to have the shareholders purchase the life insurance outside of the corporation, be the owners and beneficiaries of the policies, and at the time of need, contribute or lend the proceeds to the corporation. Premiums could be paid via a split dollar or IRC Section 162 bonus plan. Additional insurance could be purchased in anticipation of the alternative minimum tax. Finally, corporate purchases of life insurance could be made in the original needed amount and if the alternative minimum tax applies, there would be a shortfall in the amount of the tax. This shortfall could be made up in various ways, such as out of current earnings or by loans.

There are several factors which come into play as to whether or not the alternative minimum tax is applicable (i.e. the presence of a particular tax preference, adjustments to items of taxable income, the current corporate tax, timing of the insured's death, and whether the $40,000 alternative minimum tax exemption is applicable).

9. Income Taxation of Life Insurance Trust

The typical life insurance trust is unfunded and produces no income. Therefore, in the usual case, it is of no consequence to determine whether the trust is a separate income tax entity or whether the grantor or others (if substantial owners) would have income, deductions and credits of the trust attributable to them under the grantor trust rules of IRC Sections 671 through 679. However, should the trust be funded, this question would have to be resolved although, after the TRA 86, the incentive to shelter income in an irrevocable trust is diluted because of the compression of the trust income tax brackets. Even if the trust is not funded and produces no current income, the applicability of the grantor trust rules can still be of importance in determining wheher the grantor or the trust is able to deduct interest on loans against cash value of insurance policies (the defective trust) or whether the beneficiary who allows a Crummey power to lapse is to be treated as a substantial owner of the portion of the trust affected by the lapse under IRC Section 678 if and when the trust produces income at a future date (e.g., investment of life insurance proceeds after the death of the insured).

a. Grantor Trust Rules. Clearly the income from a funded life insurance trust will be taxed to the grantor of the trust if the grantor retains a reversionary interest in excess of 5% except in certain cases where the reversion is limited to the death of a trust beneficiary before twenty-one years of age if he is a minor descendant of the grantor (IRC Section 673), the grantor retains certain powers to control the beneficial enjoyment of the trust property without the approval or consent of any adverse party (IRC Section 674), the retention of certain administrative powers over trust property

(IRC Section 675) or the power of the grantor or a nonadverse party to revoke the trust (IRC Section 676). However, since most life insurance trusts are established in order to remove the insurance proceeds from the estate of the insured grantor, these types of powers would not be retained over such a trust since they would generally result in inclusion of the insurance proceeds in the grantor's gross estate. However, some of the powers included in IRC Section 677 could trigger the inclusion of trust income in the gross income of the grantor without necessarily including the assets of the trust in the grantor's gross estate for estate tax purposes.

(1) Income for the Benefit of the Grantor - IRC Section 677. This section of the Code includes in the gross income of the grantor the trust income from that portion of the trust which, without the approval or consent of an adverse party, may be (a) distributed to the grantor or the grantor's spouse, (b) held or accumulated for future distribution to the grantor or the grantor's spouse, or (c) applied to the payment of premiums on policies of insurance on the life of the grantor or the grantor's spouse unless the policy is irrevocably payable to a charity. The provisions of Section 677 apply if the trust income may be used for these purposes although it is not actually used for these purposes except, if income of the trust may be used to discharge a legal obligation of support by the grantor of someone other than the grantor's spouse, trust income will be included in the grantor's gross income only to the extent the income is actually used to discharge such legal obligation of support. Normally, in order to prevent inclusion of the insurance proceeds in the grantor's gross estate under IRC Section 2036, the grantor is not directly or indirectly a beneficiary of an irrevocable life insurance trust. However, it is possible to have the spouse of the grantor as a beneficiary or to have the trust income pay premiums on policies on the life of the grantor or the grantor's spouse without inclusion of the insurance proceeds in the grantor's gross estate.

(2) Trust Income May Be Used To Pay Premiums. Unless the policy is irrevocably payable to a charity or the payment of premiums

is subject to the approval of an adverse party, the grantor is taxed on the portion of the income of the trust that may be applied to the payment of premiums on policies of insurance on the life of the grantor or the grantor's spouse. IRC Section 677(a)(3). The statute applies whether the policy is transferred to the trust by the grantor or the trustee subsequently purchased the policy on the grantor's life. *Arthur Stockstrom*, 3 T.C. 664 (1944). Even though trust income was not used to pay the premiums on insurance policies owned by the trust, the grantor will still be taxed on trust income up to the amount of premium payable on the policy if the trustee had the discretion to apply the trust income to the payment of premiums. The statute cannot be avoided merely by having the trust instrument specify that premium payments will be made out of corpus rather than trust income. P.L.R. 8839008. Reg. Sec. 1.67-2(b).

If the trust owns no existing policies on the life of the grantor or the grantor's spouse upon which premiums might be paid and no part of the trust income is used for that purpose, the grantor trust rules do not apply, even though the trust instrument permits payment of insurance premiums. *Corning v. Commissioner*, 104 F.2d 329 (6th Cir. 1939). Presumably, even if the trust did not own a policy on the life of the grantor or the grantor's spouse, the direct payment of such premium on a policy owned by a third party or an explicit direction in the trust instrument authorizing the payment of the premium on such a third party-owned policy would trigger the grantor trust rules of Section 677(a)(3). If the trust beneficiary voluntarily uses distributions from the trust to pay premiums on an insurance policy on the grantor's life owned by the beneficiary, none of the trust income is taxable to the grantor. *Lewis Barker*, 2 T.C.M. 797 (1943). However, if there is an understanding or arrangement between the grantor and the trust beneficiary that the latter will use distributions from the trust to pay premiums on a policy on the grantor's life, then the trust income up to the amount of such premium payments will be taxable to the grantor. *L.B. Foster*, 8 T.C. 197 (1947).

Under the terms of Section 677(a)(3), the grantor trust rules would not apply to a trust which owns a policy on the life of someone other than the grantor or the grantor's spouse (e.g., a grandfather creating a trust for grandchildren with a policy on the life of his child). *Commissioner v. Jergens*, 127 F.2d 973 (5th Cir. 1942). This would not be true, however, if the nominal grantor created the trust with funds provided by the insured with the understanding that the funds would be used to establish an irrevocable life insurance trust. *Lorenz Iversen*, 3 T.C. 756 (1944).

(3) Grantor's Spouse as Trust Beneficiary. If the grantor's spouse is a beneficiary of a funded irrevocable life insurance trust, then the income of the trust will be taxable to the grantor under IRC Section 677(a)(2).

b. Crummey Withdrawal Powers. The Crummey withdrawal power is a very popular device for converting gifts to an irrevocable life insurance trust from future interest gifts to present interest gifts qualifying them for the gift tax annual exclusion. However, in regard to a funded irrevocable life insurance trust, the existence of a Crummey withdrawal power will have an income tax impact on the beneficiary possessing the power under the grantor trust rules and such beneficiary may have a continuing income tax impact even after the Crummey powers have lapsed.

(1) Crummey Withdrawal Powers Before Lapse. The Crummey withdrawal right of a beneficiary constitutes "a power exercisable solely by himself to vest the corpus in himself" which will cause him to be treated as the owner of the portion of the trust subject to the withdrawal power. IRC Section 678(a)(1). P.L.R. 8142061. P.L.R. 8308033. P.L.R. 8342088. This is true even though the beneficiary is a minor without a legally appointed guardian. Rev. Rul. 81-6, 1981-1 C.B. 385. During the tax year that the withdrawal power exists, the beneficiary will include a pro rata portion of all income, deductions and credits of the trust equal to a fraction, the numerator of which is the dollar amount subject to the withdrawal and the denominator of which is the fair market value of the trust property at the date the withdrawal

expressly state that the lapse of a general power of appointment shall be considered a release of such power for estate and gift tax purposes. IRC Sections 2041(b)(2) and 2514(e). Presumably, the failure of Congress to so state for income tax purposes is an indication that Congress did not intend for a "lapse" to be considered a "release" for the grantor trust rules.

Under Section 678(b), if the grantor of the insurance trust is treated as the owner under the grantor trust rules, the beneficiaries possessing the Crummey withdrawal power will not be subject to the grantor trust rules, (e.g., a defective trust where trust income may be used to pay premiums under Section 677(a)(3)). P.L.R. 8517052. In the case of a funded irrevocable life insurance trust, Section 678(b) would not be useful since the trust income would be taxable to the grantor. However, in the case of an unfunded irrevocable life insurance trust which produces no income, there would be no adverse income tax consequences to the grantor because of Section 678(b) and the beneficiaries would be protected from income tax consequences after the death of the insured grantor when the insurance proceeds are invested by the trust to produce income.

10. Split Dollar Life Insurance

A split dollar plan is a versatile method to finance premium payments on a permanent life insurance policy, presumably including universal and variable life policies (although there are no rulings on point). Split dollar is used in any situation where one party has a life insurance need and another party has the ability to pay the premiums. Two parties agree to split the ownership and the benefits of a policy. One party obtains needed life insurance protection and the other party helps by paying all or a portion of the premiums. The premium payor will usually be secured for the premium payments by the policy's cash value and death benefit.

A split dollar plan could arise between a parent and child, a grandparent and a grandchild or between business partners. But, split dollar is used most often in an employer-employee setting, in which the employer helps a key employee obtain permanent life insurance protection by making the premium payments.

There are three methods which may be used to enumerate ownership rights in a split dollar plan: the endorsement method, the collateral assignment method and the split ownership method. The endorsement method whereby the employer is the owner provides maximum security for premium payments. The rights of the parties are listed or endorsed on the life insurance policy. The collateral assignment method uses the policy itself as security for the premium payments with the insured as policy owner. Split ownership permits parties to apportion policy ownership in any desired manner.

a. Income Tax Treatment To The Insured. Death proceeds are received income tax free. IRC Section 101(a). Rev. Rul. 64-328, 1964-2 C.B. 11.

In family split dollar, there should be no income tax consequences resulting from the payment of premiums or receipt of benefits since no employment or shareholder relationship is involved.

In the business setting, taxable income can arise from three different sources: the economic benefit, any bonuses and dividends. The economic benefit is based on the cost of pure insurance protection provided by the employer's premium payment. It is reportable as income to the employee each year. If the employee contributes to the premium, the contribution reduces the amount of taxable income dollar for dollar. While the split dollar plan remains in effect, the employee must report an economic benefit even if no more premium payments are payable. Rev. Rul. 64-328, *supra*.

The value of the economic benefit is determined by multiplying the employee's share of the death benefit by the government's one-year term rates (P.S. 58 cost table) as provided in Rev. Rul. 55-747, 1955-2 C.B. 228. However, Rev. Rul. 66-110, 1966-2 C.B. 11 states that if the "current published premium rates per $1,000 of insurance protection charged by an insurer for individual one-year term life insurance available to all standard risks are lower than those set forth in Rev. Rul. 55-747, such published rates may be used in place of the rates set forth in that revenue ruling for determining the cost of insurance in connection with individual policies issued by the same insurer and used for split dollar arrangements." Note that the standard term rates of the carrier issuing the split dollar policy must be used in determining the

c. Income Tax Treatment To The Premium Payer. Any premium payments made by the premium payer (including any economic benefit realized by the employee as income) are not income tax deductible to the employer, because of the prohibition of IRC Section 264(a)(1) of a deduction for premium payments if the employer is directly or indirectly a beneficiary under the policy. Rev. Rul. 64-328, *supra*. In the business setting, if the employer pays the employee a bonus to offset all or a portion of the employee's cost, the bonus is income tax deductible by the employer if the total compensation is deemed reasonable. IRC Section 162(a)(i). However, if the bonus is closely tied to the employee's portion of the premium payment, there could be a danger that the IRS will disallow the deduction.

Any cash value received by the premium payer at the time of a rollout is exempt from federal income taxes as long as it does not exceed the premium payer's total premium contributions. IRC Section 72. Death proceeds are received income tax free. Rev. Rul. 64-328, *supra*.

d. Transfer For Value. A transfer for value of a life insurance contract may result in income taxation of the death benefits (in excess of premiums and other consideration paid) unless one of the statutory exceptions is met. IRC Section 101(a)(2). Most split dollar agreements give the owner of the pure insurance portion the right to purchase the employer's investment element upon rollout. Such a purchase would literally appear to be a transfer for value if the owner is not one of the enumerated statutory exceptions: the insured, the insured's partner or partnership, a corporation of which he is an officer or a shareholder, or the transferee receives a carryover basis on the transfer. IRC Section 101(a)(2)(B). Other third parties in split dollar plans are the insured's children, an irrevocable life insurance trust and a co-shareholder. Transfers from the employer to these third parties are not exempt from the transfer for value rule.

If a collateral assignment split dollar format is used, the form would not indicate a transfer on its surface upon termination of the plan. The third party owner would pay off the employer for his "loans" by borrowing against the cash value at the date of plan termination. However, the IRS might still treat this as a transfer because of its stated position that there is no loan but an investment by the employer in the policy regardless of whether an endorsement or collateral assignment format is used.

Some argue that a policy subject to a split ownership method creates a stronger argument against transfer for value at rollout since the contract shows separate ownership interests on its face. However, unless separate ownership is construed by the IRS to mean separate policies, the transfer for value rule would apply to a joint ownership contract since the transfer for value rule applies to transfers of all or part of the proceeds of a single life insurance policy. Reg. Sec. 1.101-1(b)(4).

e. Reverse Split Dollar. In reverse split dollar, the usual split of the policy is reversed. The employer owns the risk element and the employee owns the cash value. The premiums may be split or the employer may pay the entire premium. A common method is to have the employee pay the premiums and the employer to contribute the economic benefit costs. In essence, the employer receives a key person death benefit under this plan. Ownership is usually arranged so that the employee is the policy owner. The employee endorses the employer's interest in the cash value and death benefit to the employer.

To date, the tax consequences of reverse split dollar are not clear because there are no statutes, cases, rulings or regulations. Some reverse split dollar proposals attempt to create a tax leverage in favor of the employee by having the employer measure the economic benefit of the risk element by the higher P.S. 58 cost table in Rev. Rul. 55-747, *supra*, rather than the lower insurance carrier term rate table. The use of the higher P.S. 58 cost table in many cases results in the employer paying all or most of the annual premium on the policy. For a traditional split dollar arrangement, Rev. Rul. 64-328 and Rev. Rul. 66-110 stated that the economic benefit of the at risk element to the employee could be measured by either the P.S. 58 cost table or the insurance carrier's term rate if lower. It is unknown whether the IRS will allow the same taxpayer discretion in measuring economic benefit under a reverse split dollar contract where the employer is the owner of the at risk element. The IRS might argue that this is not a split dollar arrangement subject to

that a pension plan provide definitely determinable benefits. Rev. Rul. 69-523, 1969-2 C.B. 90. However, a profit sharing plan is able to invest part of a participant's account in life insurance on the life of another. P.L.R. 8426090.

b. Incidental Death Benefit Rule. The IRS has developed the 25%/50% test in determining whether life insurance purchased by a qualified benefit plan provides an incidental death benefit. There is an alternative 100 times test which may be used by defined benefit plans (and in some rare instances, a defined contribution plan) in meeting the incidental death benefit rule.

(1) 25%/50% Test. In relation to a profit sharing plan which owns a whole life policy allocated to the account of the insured employee, the incidental death benefit rule is met if less than 50% of the contributions and forfeitures allocated to such account is used to pay premiums on such policy and if the trustee is required at the employee's retirement to either convert the policy at or before retirement to provide periodic income so that no portion of the value may be used to continue life insurance protection beyond retirement or to distribute the contract to the employee at retirement. Rev. Rul. 60-84, 1960-1 C.B. 159.

If only term insurance has been purchased and allocated to the employee's profit sharing account, then the premium payment cannot exceed 25% of the annual contributions and forfeitures allocated to that account. If both whole life and term insurance are allocated to the employee's profit sharing plan account, then one-half of the annual whole life premium plus the total term premium cannot in the aggregate exceed 25% of the contributions and forfeitures allocated to that account during the year. Rev. Rul. 61-164, 1961-2 C.B. 99. The same rules apply to a money purchase pension plan. Rev. Rul. 66-143, 1966-1 C.B. 79. Actually, the 50% portion of the test is really a variation of the 25% test since the rulings state the IRS assumption that approximately one-half of the premium paid on a whole life policy provides current insurance protection while the remaining half accrues in the cash surrender value. If a defined contribution plan meets the 25%/50% test, the beneficiaries at the death of the employee can receive both the death benefit under the insurance policy and the balance of other assets in the deceased employee's account without disqualifying the plan. Rev. Rul. 73-501, 1973-2 C.B. 127. The 25%/50% test may be applied to a defined benefit pension plan where the cost of the insurance and all other death benefits under the plan may not exceed the stated percentage in comparison to the cost of all benefits provided under the plan. Rev. Rul. 70-611, 1970-2 C.B. 89.

What is the distinguishing feature between a whole life policy and a term policy? The IRS position is that a whole life policy has a level amount of insurance for life with a level premium payment. Thus, a whole life policy with a decreasing amount of insurance coverage for ten years with a level premium was treated as a term policy subject to the 25% test. Rev. Rul. 76-353, 1976-2 C.B. 112. Likewise, where the policy had a level premium but it was a combination of whole life and term coverage with the term part decreasing each year in the amount of paid up additions purchased with dividends from the whole life portion of the policy, the IRS ruled that this was a term policy subject to the 25% test since it was not practicable to split the annual premium between the term coverage and the whole life coverage. P.L.R. 8029100. On the other hand, where a flexible premium adjustable life policy was involved which could result in either term coverage or whole life coverage because of changing the face amount of the policy or the premium, the IRS ruled that the 50% test would apply in any year that the policy qualified as whole life and the 25% test in any year that the policy qualified as term since, at any particular time actuarial calculations could determine whether the plan of insurance at that time was term protection or whole life protection. P.L.R. 8725088. Apparently, a flexible premium universal life policy will be treated by the IRS as a term policy subject to the 25% test since the Service so states in Document Provision 65 in its package of suggested plan provisions for defined contribution master or prototype plans.

by the employee towards the premium payment. Reg. Sec. 1.72-16(b)(4). The lump sum payment of the cash value portion could also qualify for the special $5,000 employee death benefit exclusion. IRC Section 101(b)(2)(B)(i).

Where the employer, the insured employee or the trustee of another plan transfer an insurance policy on the life of the employee to the trustee of a qualified pension or profit sharing plan, there is no transfer for value since the insured retains the right to designate the beneficiary of the insurance proceeds and is the recipient of the cash value of the policy upon retirement. Rev. Rul. 73-338, 1973-2 C.B. 20. Rev. Rul. 74-76, 1974-1 C.B. 30. P.L.R. 7844032.

If the insurance proceeds are payable in installments, the cash surrender value portion will be taxed in the same manner as any installment payments from a qualified pension or profit sharing plan. For the amount of the insurance proceeds in excess of the cash surrender value, they will be taxed under IRC Section 101(d). *See* item 2.c.

e. Taxation of Policy Upon Severance From Employment. If a life insurance policy is distributed from the plan to the insured employee, the entire cash value of the contract at the time of distribution (less any basis attributable to P.S. 58 cost, employee premium payments, etc.) is includable in the employee's income unless, within 60 days after the distribution of such contract, all or any portion of such value is irrevocably converted into an annuity contract with no life insurance element. Reg. Sec. 1.402(a)-1(a)(2). Another way to avoid income taxation of the cash surrender value is to roll over the policy to another trust qualified under 401(a) or an annuity plan qualified under 403(a) within 60 days of the distribution. IRC Secton 402(a)(5).

However, a life insurance policy may not be rolled over to an IRA. Rev. Rul. 81-275, 1981-2 C.B. 92. The employee can indirectly roll the cash value of the insurance policy over to an IRA by using one of several techniques. He could purchase the insurance policy from the employee benefit trust in an amount equal to its cash value and then roll the distribution (which includes the sales proceeds) to the IRA. P.L.R. 7829152. The plan trustee could surrender the policy and the employee could roll over the distribution (which includes the policy surrender proceeds) to an IRA. Finally, the trustee could take a maximum loan against the cash value of the insurance policy, distribute the policy and the other assets (which include the proceeds of the loan) to the employee who rolls over the entire distribution except the insurance policy to the IRA. P.L.R. 7727003.

f. Prohibited Transaction Rules. As mentioned earlier, it is sometimes desirable for the pension or profit sharing plan to sell an insurance policy owned by the plan to the insured or some other person exempt from the transfer for value rule. For example, the employee might now be non-insurable and wish to have this existing insurance policy for personal or business use. Also, in order for an amount equal to the cash surrender value to be eligible for a roll over to an IRA, it may be desirable for the employee to purchase the policy from the plan for an amount equal to its cash surrender value. A transfer of the policy without a purchase would be considered a taxable distribution. It may also be desirable for a plan to purchase an existing policy from the insured employee rather than purchasing a new policy.

Anytime the insurance policies or other assets are purchased by a qualified plan from or sold by a qualified plan to an employee, one must be mindful of the prohibited transaction rules of the Internal Revenue Code and ERISA. The law imposes an annual 5% excise tax on a disqualified person of the amount involved with respect to a prohibited transaction with a qualified plan. If the prohibited transaction is not corrected within a certain period of time, there can be an additional 100% excise tax. IRC Section 4975(a) and (b). There are two prohibited transactions pertinent to our purposes. The first is a sale or exchange of any property between a plan and a disqualified person and the second is a transfer to a disqualified person of the income or assets of the plan. IRC Section 4975(c)(1)(A) and (D).

The prohibited transaction rules only apply to sales to or purchases from a disqualified person. Just because the insured is an employee of the plan sponsor and a participant in the plan does not make him a disqualified person. Examples of disqualified persons in the situation of a sale or purchase of a life insurance policy by or to a qualified plan include a person who owns 50% or more of an ownership interest distribution (which includes the policy surrender proceeds) to an IRA. Finally, the trustee could take a maximum loan against the cash value of the insurance policy, distribute the policy and the other assets (which include the proceeds of the loan) to the employee who rolls over the entire distribution except the insurance policy to the IRA. P.L.R. 7727003.

Prohibited Transaction Rules. As mentioned earlier, it is sometimes desirable for the pension or profit sharing plan to sell an insurance policy owned by the plan to the insured or some other person exempt from the prohibited transaction rules. For example, the employee might now be non-insurable and wish to have this existing insurance policy for personal tax purposes. Also, in order for an amount equal to the cash surrender value to be eligible for a roll over to an IRA, it may be desirable for the employee to purchase the policy from the plan for an amount equal to its cash surrender value. A transfer of the policy without a purchase would be considered a taxable distribution. It may also be desirable for a plan to purchase an existing policy from the insured employee rather than purchasing a new policy.

Assuming the insurance policies or other assets are purchased by a qualified plan from or sold by a qualified plan to an employee, one must be mindful of the prohibited transaction rules of the Internal Revenue Code and ERISA. The law imposes a 5% annual excise tax on a disqualified person on the amount involved with respect to a prohibited transaction with a qualified plan. If the prohibited transaction is not corrected within a certain period of time, there can be an additional 100% excise tax. IRC Section 4975(a) and (b). There are two prohibited transactions pertinent to our purposes. The first is a sale or exchange of any property between a plan and a disqualified person and the second is a transfer to a disqualified person of the income or assets of the plan. IRC Section 4975(c)(1)(A) and (D).

The prohibited transaction rules only apply to sales to or purchases from a disqualified person. Just because the insured is an employee of the plan sponsor and a participant in the plan does not make him a disqualified person. Examples of disqualified persons in the situation of a sale or purchase of a life insurance policy by or to a qualified plan include a person who owns 50% or more of an ownership interest for the sale, be surrendered by the plan, if the policy is to be sold to someone other than the participant-insured, the participant is given the option to purchase the policy and must consent in writing to the sale, the purchase price must be at least equal to the cash surrender value and the sale does not discriminate in form or operation in favor of plan participants who are officers, shareholders or highly compensated employees.

12. Group Term Life Insurance.

If certain statutory rules are met, the cost of up to $50,000 of group term insurance coverage provided by an employer for active or retired employees may be excluded from the employee's income. In the case of a disabled employee, the entire group term insurance coverage provided by the employer (without regard to the $50,000 ceiling) may be excluded from his or her gross income. Special income inclusion rules apply to highly compensated employees for group term insurance plans that discriminate in their favor.

a. Formal Plan Requirements. ERISA has long required that any employee benefit plan (which includes a group term life insurance plan) be established and maintained pursuant to a written instrument, which provides for one or more named fiduciaries who shall have the authority to control and manage the operation and administration of the plan. The document must also provide a procedure for amending the plan and specify the basis on which payments are to be made to and from the plan. ERISA Sec. 402. In addition, every group term life insurance plan must provide adequate notice in writing to any participant or beneficiary whose claims for benefits under the plan have been denied, setting forth the specific reasons for such denial, written in a manner calculated to be understood by the participant, and the plan shall afford a reasonable opportunity to any participant whose claims for benefits has been denied for a full and fair review by the appropriate named fiduciary of the decision denying the claim. ERISA Sec. 503.

If assets are set aside by the employer (e.g., to fund post-retirement group term insurance), ERISA requires that such assets be held in a trust by one or more trustees, either named in the trust instrument or in the plan instrument or appointed by the fiduciary. ERISA Sec. 403. The trust instrument must be in writing and expressly provide that the trustee is subject to the direction of the fiduciary. ERISA Reg. Sec. 2550.403a-1. The trust requirement does not apply if the assets consist of insurance contracts or such assets are held by an insurance company. ERISA Reg. Sec. 403(b)(1)-(2). Effective August 15, 1988, any employee contributions received or withheld by the employer for group term life insurance premiums (or dependent life insurance premiums) are considered plan assets and must be transferred to a trust as of the earliest date on which such contributions can reasonably be segregated from the employer's general assets. ERISA Sec. 2510.3-102. Pending a review of the particular problems involving cafeteria plans, employee contributions to group term insurance coverage through such plans will not have to be segregated into a separate trust. ERISA Technical Release 88-1, August 12, 1988.

Starting with plan years beginning after 1988, the Internal Revenue Code imposes its own formal requirement on group term life insurance plans. IRC Sections 89(k) and 89(i)(1)(B). Except to the extent provided in regulations, (1) the plan must be in writing, (2) the employee's rights must be legally enforceable, (3) employees must be given reasonable notification of plan benefits, (4) the plan must be maintained for the exclusive benefit of the employees and (5) the plan is intended to be maintained for an indefinite period of time. IRC Section 89(k)(1). A plan is not legally enforceable if it is discretionary with the employer, but a plan will not fail to satisfy the legally enforceable requirement merely because the employer has the right to terminate the plan with respect to claims not yet incurred. Conf. Rept. No. 99-841, Vol. II, p. II-504. If the plan does not meet the formal requirements, then the special income taxation rules of Section 79 are lost (e.g., exclusion of cost of the first $50,000 of coverage and the use of Table I for the excess coverage) and the value of the benefits provided by the employer will be included in the employee's gross income for the taxable year. IRC Section 89(k)(1)-(3). If the group term insurance plan discriminates in favor of highly compensated employees but also fails the formal requirements, then the highly compensated employee will realize income under Section 89(k) in lieu of income otherwise taxable to him under the nondiscrimination rules. IRC Section 89(k)(1). Although the Conference Committee Report states that the income inclusion is based upon the value of the benefits provided rather than the value of the coverage under the plan (giving an example of a health plan failing these requirements), presumably, in the case of group term life insurance, the value of the benefits and the cost of the coverage would be the same with the result that the premium payments by the employer (reduced by any employee contributions) for the entire group term insurance coverage would be includable in the employee's gross income in case of a violation of the formal requirements. *See* Conf. Rept. No. 99-841, Vol. II, p. II-504.

b. Requirements Imposed By IRC Section 79. In addition to meeting the formal requirements of Section 89(k), the group term life insurance plan must meet certain requirements imposed by the regulations under Section 79. There are four requirements under the regulations: (1) a general death benefit which meets the definition of life insurance contract, (2) provided to a group of employees, (3) under a policy carried directly or indirectly by the employer, (4) with the amount of insurance provided to each employee computed under a formula which precludes individual selection. Reg. Sec. 1.79-1(a).

(1) General Death Benefit. Since travel insurance and accident and health insurance (including amounts payable under a double indemnity clause or rider) do not provide a general death benefit, such policies do not fall within the definition of group term life insurance under Section 79. Reg. Sec. 1.79-1(f)(3). The cited regulation implies that travel insurance and accidental death insurance are subject to the income exclusion rules of IRC Section 106 for employer contributions to accident and health plans. Since accident or health plans are defined as arrangements covering personal injuries or sickness of an employee or his dependents (Reg. Secs. 1.105-5(a) and 1.016-1), there has been some doubt as to whether the death benefit portion of travel insurance or accidental death and dismemberment insurance qualified for income exclusion under Sections 105 and 106. However, in determining whether an accidental death plan fit within the definition of an accident and health plan under Section 106 for purposes of qualifying for salary reduction under a cafeteria plan, the IRS has ruled that premiums paid by employees pursuant to a salary reduction

agreement under a cafeteria plan were excluded from the employee's income under Section 106 but the ruling cautioned that it may be modified or revoked by adoption of temporary or final regulations inconsistent with the conclusions of the ruling. P.L.R. 8801015.

(2) Provided to a Group of Employees. An employee is a person who performs services within the legal relationship of employer and employee. Reg. Sec. 1.79-0. Thus Section 79 does not apply to insurance coverage provided to a corporate director, a commission salesman who is not a common-law employee, or a business owner. *Maurice Enright*, 56 T.C. 1261 (1971). Rev. Rul. 56-400, 1956-2 C.B. 116. *Whipple Chrysler-Plymouth*, 31 T.C.M. 230 (1972). Thus the self-employed including partners would not be eligible under Section 79. Shareholders of S corporations who own more than 2% of the outstanding stock or stock possessing more than 2% of the voting power are considered partners for fringe benefit purposes. IRC Section 1372. The legislative history indicates that the exclusion of the cost of up to $50,000 of group term life insurance is among the fringe benefits. A former employee is considered an "employee" if the group term insurance coverage is related to his former employment and a full-time life insurance salesperson who is considered an employee for social security tax purposes can also be covered by group term life insurance. Reg. Sec. 1.79-0. Even if the insured is an employee, Section 79 is not applicable if the group insurance is made available to him in his capacity as director or owner. *Enright*, *supra*. *Whipple Chrysler-Plymouth*, *supra*. Group insurance for dependents is not covered since they are not employees. Reg. Sec. 1.79-3(f)(2).

Not only must the insurance be made available to an employee it must also be provided to a group of employees. Normally, the group of employees is all of the employees of an employer or less than all employees if membership in the group is determined solely on the basis of age, marital status or factors related to employment. Except as noted below, a group of employees must include ten or more full-time employees at some time during the calendar year. Examples of factors relating to employment which may be considered in not covering all of the employees are union membership, duties performed, compensation received, length of service, or participation in the employer's pension, profit sharing or accident and health plans. Ordinarily, the purchase of something other than group term life insurance (e.g. employer provided credit life insurance to employees who purchase automobiles) is not a factor related to employment. Stock ownership in the employer corporation is not a factor related to employment except that participation in the employer's stock bonus plan may be such a factor. Reg. Sec. 1.79-0.

As indicated above, normally Section 79 does not apply to a group term insurance plan which has not provided at least ten employees at some time during a calendar year. In determining the number of employees, all life insurance provided under policies carried directly or indirectly by the employer is taken into account and insurance is considered provided to an employee who elects not to receive the insurance unless the employee is required to contribute to the cost of benefits other than just term life insurance (e.g., permanent insurance coverage). Reg. Secs. 1.79-1(c)(1) and (5). If less than ten employees are provided insurance, Section 79 can still apply to a group term life insurance plan if the additional requirements of one of the following two tests are met:

(a) The conditions of the first test are as follows: (i) the insurance is provided to all full-time employees, who provide satisfactory evidence of insurability, (ii) the amount of insurance is computed either as a uniform percentage of compensation or on the basis of coverage brackets under which no bracket is more than 2 1/2 times the next lower bracket and the lowest bracket is at least 10% of the highest bracket (the insurer may establish a separate set of 2 1/2 times/10% coverage brackets for those who are over age 65), and (iii) evidence of insurability is limited to a medical questionnaire and does not require a physical examination. Reg. Sec.

1.79-1(c)(2). An under ten plan is considered to provide insurance to an employee who declines coverage if he is not required as a condition of coverage to contribute to the cost of any benefit other than group term life insurance. Reg. Sec. 1.79-1(c)(5). Even though an under ten plan contains brackets meeting the 2 1/2 times/10% test, brackets will be ignored if they are artificially drawn and are never or seldom used. Rev. Rul. 80-220, 1980-2 C.B. 35. Since the regulations require the brackets to be set by the insurer, a group term plan is disqualified under Section 79 if the brackets are set by the corporate officers. *Ronald Gene Braswell*, 42 T.C.M. 1053 (1981). Although the regulations state that a medical questionnaire may only be used in determining an employee's "eligibility for insurance or the amount of insurance provided," the IRS has ruled that a medical examination is also prohibited in determining the cost of a group term insurance premium after eligibility and the amount of insurance have been determined pursuant to a questionnaire. Rev. Rul. 75-528, 1975-2 C.B. 35.

(b) The conditions of the second test for an under ten plan are usually met by small union plans: (i) the insurance is provided under a common plan to employees of two or more unrelated employers, (ii) the insurance is restricted to, but mandatory for, all employees of the employer who are represented by an organization (such as a union) that carries on substantial activities in addition to obtaining insurance, and (iii) evidence of insurability is not required for eligibility or the amount of insurance.

(c) In applying either of the two above tests, the following employees may be excluded in determining whether all employees are provided coverage: (i) employees ineligible because of a waiting period specified in the policy up to six months, (ii) employees whose customary employment is for not more than 20 hours in any week or five months in any calendar year, and (iii) employees who have reached the age of 65. Note that an employee need not be counted if he voluntarily waives coverage for the first test but such a waiver will disqualify application of the second test since it is mandatory that all employees be covered.

(d) Since all group term plans are aggregated in determining whether fewer than ten employees are provided group term insurance, it is possible to superimpose on a basic group term life insurance plan providing coverage to ten or more employees another group term plan providing additional coverage for a select group of employees which may number less than ten without having to comply with the special rules for under ten plans. However, the superimposed coverage must still meet the requirement of Section 79 precluding individual selection and the nondiscrimination in favor of highly compensated employees under Section 89.

(3) Policy Carried Directly or Indirectly by the Employer. The term "policy" includes two or more obligations of an insurer (or its affiliates) that are sold in conjunction, that is, they are offered or available because of the employment relationship. Thus group insurance can be in the form of a master contract or individual policies. Obligations are sold in conjunction without regard to the actuarial sufficiency of a premium charge for each obligation, whether the obligations are contained in separate documents, whether each document is filed with an approved by the applicable state insurance commission or whether each obligation is independent of any other obligations. However, an employer may elect to treat two or more obligations each of which provides no permanent benefits as separate policies if the premiums are properly allocated among such policies. Reg. Sec. 1.79-0.

The policy is "carried directly or indirectly" by an employer if either the employer pays any part of the cost of life insurance directly or through another person or the employer arranges for payment of the cost of the insurance by the employees and charges at least one employee less than the Table I cost and at least one other employee more than the Table I cost. Reg. Sec. 1.79-0. Thus, it is possible to have a policy carried directly or indirectly by an employer where the entire costs are paid by the employees if the Table I cost of at least one employee's coverage is provided by the contributions of at least one other employee, e.g., each employee pays a level contribution. Supplementary group coverage totally paid for by the employees will be subject to Section 79 if the basic group term insurance is paid all in part by the employer and both policies are issued by this same insurance carrier. However, where the supplemental group insurance paid for by the employees is issued by a different insurance carrier from the one who issues the basic group term insurance coverage, the supplemental coverage will not be subject to Section 79. P.L.R. 8129070. P.L.R. 8518037.

(4) Insurance Computed Under a Formula That Precludes Individual Selection. Since under ten plans must have coverage brackets, this requirement applies to ten or more employee plans. The formula must be based on factors such as age, years of service, compensation, or position. This condition may be satisfied even if the amount of insurance provided is determined under a limited number of alternative schedules that are based on the amount each employee elects to contribute, e.g., the employee may elect to purchase supplemental group coverage at his own expense. However, the amount of insurance provided under each schedule must be computed under a formula that precludes individual selection. Reg. Sec. 1.79-1(a)(4). Even if there is a formula based upon years of service or position, Section 79 will not apply if the facts show that the formula was drawn to provide extra insurance coverage to a particular person such as a president or former president. *William Towne*, 78 T.C. 791 (1982). *Arthur Whitcomb*, 81 T.C. 505 (1983), aff'd on another issue, 733 F.2d 191 (1st Cir. 1984). However, if a certain amount of insurance was made available for the position of officer and several individuals fell within this category, the formula was determined to preclude individual selection. *NWD Investment Co.*, 44 T.C.M. 1246 (1982). If the amount of group term coverage is reduced by any death benefit payable from the

employer's pension plan, Section 79 is not applicable since the formula for determining the amount of life insurance coverage is based upon factors other than age, years of service, compensation or position. P.L.R. 8342008. The IRS will not issue rulings as to whether group term insurance for ten or more employees qualifies under Section 79 unless the requirements (brackets) for under ten employee plans are applicable to the particular plan. Rev. Proc. 88-3, Sec. 3.01(1), 1988-1 I.R.B. 29. Even before the ruling moratorium, there was some concern that the IRS was over emphasizing the brackets for ten and over groups in determining what factors may preclude individual selection. *See* T.A.M. 7852013 and T.A.M. 8014003. Even if the requirements of a formula that precludes individual selection are met, a group term insurance plan will still have to meet the nondiscrimination requirements of Section 89 to preclude income taxation to highly compensated employees.

(5) Combined With a Permanent Benefit. Actually, there is a fifth requirement that a group term life insurance contract has to meet in complying with Section 79 although regulations provide a means to avoid the requirement. No part of the life insurance provided under the policy can provide a permanent benefit unless (a) the policy or the employer designates in writing the part of the benefit that is group term life insurance and (b) the part of the benefit which is group term life insurance is not less than the total death benefit less the employee's deemed death benefit provided under the permanent insurance coverage. Reg. Sec. 1.79-1(b).

Under the regulations, a "permanent benefit" is an economic value extending beyond one policy year. Examples are paid-up or cash surrender value benefits. However, a conversion right, the provision of term insurance on level premiums for a period of five years or less, or any other feature that provides no economic benefit other than current insurance protection is not a permanent benefit. Reg. Sec. 1.79-0.

In determining whether a policy provides a permanent benefit, the same broad aggregation rule as applied to separate group term policies apply to group term and permanent policies sold in conjunction with each other because of the employment relationship. Thus, separate policies of term insurance and permanent insurance provided by an employer to a group of employees will be treated as one policy even though one of the policies is provided only to employees who decline the other policy. The employer may elect to avoid the aggregation of a separate permanent benefit policy with group term policies if: (a) the insured sells the policy directly to the employee who pays the full cost thereof; (b) the participation of the employer is limited to the selection of the insurer and the type of coverage and to sales assistance activities; (c) the insurer sells the policy on the same terms and in substantial amounts to individuals who do not purchase (and whose employers to not purchase) any other policies from the insurer; and (d) no employer provided benefit is conditioned on the purchase of the permanent policy. Reg. Sec. 1.79-0. Even if the combination of the permanent benefit with the group term life insurance is permissible because of the designation in writing of the part of the death benefit provided to the employee which is group term life insurance, the cost of the permanent benefits reduced by the amount paid by the employee for such benefits is includable in the employee's income.

The regulations contain a formula for determining the cost of the permanent benefit. Reg. Sec. 1.79-1(d). An insurance company may ask the IRS for a determination of the cost of permanent benefits and of the deemed death benefit provided by a combination group term and permanent benefit life insurance policy. The IRS will issue the ruling to an individual employer if it is not feasible for the insurance carrier to obtain the ruling. Rev. Proc. 79-29, 1979-1 C.B. 571. If dividends are paid on the permanent benefits, the employee will realize income on the dividends actually or constructively received by the employee reduced pursuant to a formula contained in the regulations if the employee contributes to the cost of the permanent benefits. Reg. Sec. 1.79-1(d)(5).

(6) State Law Limits. Section 79 does not apply to life insurance in excess of the limits under applicable state law on the amount of life insurance that can be provided to an employee under a single contract of group term life insurance. Reg. Sec. 1.79-1(e). Thus, even if the group term insurance policy meets all the other requirements of Section 79, the cost of any coverage provided in excess of the state ceiling on group insurance would be includable in the employee's income.

c. Inclusion of Group Term Insurance Coverage in Employee's Income. *See* Item No. 6 for a discussion of the income inclusion rules under Section 79 for a plan which is nondiscriminatory.

d. Highly Compensated Employees and the Nondiscrimination Rules of Section 89. The new nondiscrimination rules for group term life insurance under Section 89 go into effect for plan years beginning after 1988. For plan years beginning before 1989, a group term insurance plan which discriminated in favor of key employees resulted in the inclusion in the income of all key employees covered by the plan of the cost of the first $50,000 of insurance coverage measured by the greater of the actual premiums paid and Table I (for plan years ending before October 23, 1986, the income inclusion was measured solely by the premiums paid). Key employee had the same definition as for top-heavy purposes. A plan discriminated in favor of a key employee unless it met one of the following four tests: the plan benefited 70% or more of all employees, at least 85% of all employees who are participants are not key employees, the plan benefits a reasonable classification which does not discriminate in favor of key employees or the plan meets the cafeteria plan requirements. In running these tests, employees with less than three years of service, who are part-time or seasonal, who are covered by certain collective bargaining agreements or who are non-resident aliens with no U.S. earned income may be excluded. In addition, all plan benefits available to key employees must also be available to other plan participants but it is permissible to have a plan where the amount of group term life insurance bears the uniform relationship to total compensation of each employee. IRC Section 79(d).

Under the new Section 89 rules, if a group term life insurance plan discriminates in favor of a highly compensated employee, such employee will include in his taxable income the value of the discriminatory portion of the benefit. Highly compensated employee has the same definition as for qualified plan purposes. IRC Sections 89(j)(1) and 414(q).

In order to be nondiscriminatory, a group life insurance plan must meet a separate eligibility test and benefits test or a single alternative coverage test. In running the discrimination tests, each option or benefit offered to an employee is treated as a separate plan. IRC Section 89(j)(11). However, a group term insurance plan is not treated as two or more separate plans merely because the amount of life insurance under the plan bears a uniform relationship to compensation. IRC Section 89(j)(4)(A). However, if two types of group term insurance policies vary in any way (including the amount of employee contribution), they will be considered as separate plans.

Under the eligibility test (IRC Section 89(d)), the plan must meet the following requirements: (a) at least 90% of the non-highly compensated employees are eligible to participate with an employer provided benefit which is at least 50% of the largest employer provided benefit under all group life plans for highly compensated employees; (b) either at least 50% of the employees eligible are non-highly compensated or the percentage of the elibile non-highly compensated employees is at least equal to the percentage of eligible highly compensated employees; and (c) the group life plan does not contain a provision that discriminates in favor of highly compensated employees. Blue Book TRA 86 (page 786) expressly approves plans which provide coverage based on a uniform percentage of compensation.

Under the benefits test (IRC Section 89(e)), the average employer provided benefit received by non-highly compensated employees from all group life plans of the employer is at least 75% of the average employer provided benefits received by non-highly compensated employees from all group life plans of the employer.

As an alternative to both the eligibility test and the benefits test, a plan will be nondiscriminatory if it meets the following alternative tests of Section 89(f): (1) at least 80% of the non-highly compensated employees are covered by the group life insurance and (2) the plan does not contain provisions relating to eligibility which (by its terms or otherwise) discriminate in favor of highly compensated employees.

In applying the above nondiscrimination tests, the following employees may be excluded if none of the employees in the otherwise excludible category are actually covered by the plan: (1) employees with less than one year of service; (2) employees who normally work less than 17-1/2 hours per week; (3) employees who normally work not more than six months during any year; (4) employees who have not attained age 21; (5) employees covered by a collective bargaining agreement if there was good faith bargaining concerning group life benefits; and (6) non-resident aliens with no U.S. source income. If a shorter period or a lesser age is specified in the plan, such shorter period or lesser age will control for exclusion purposes. If there are several group life insurance plans, an exclusion must be applied to all such plans except for those covering employees in a separate line of business. IRC Section 89(h).

In determining the valuation of group life benefits for the discrimination test purposes, the employer provided benefit equals the value of the group term life coverage attributable to employer contributions. IRC Section 89(g)(3)(A)(i). The value of such coverage to any employee shall be determined by using the Table I cost chart as if the employee was age 40. IRC Section 89(g)(3)(C)(i). That will be 17¢ per month per $1,000 of coverage. In determining the average employer provided group life insurance benefit, the aggregate of benefits provided to all highly compensated employees under the plans shall be divided by the number of highly compensated employees (whether or not they are covered under such plans). The average employer provided benefit for non-highly compensated employees shall be determined in the same manner. IRC Section 89(e)(2).

If a group term plan is deemed discriminatory in applying a benefits test, the discriminatory excess benefit will be includable in the income of the highly compensated employee. IRC Section 89(a)(1). The excess benefit for a highly compensated employee is determined by reducing the coverage of each such employee (starting with the highly compensated employee with the highest otherwise non-taxable benefits) using the Table I rate as if the employee were 40 years of age until the plan would be nondiscriminatory. IRC Section 89(b). After the excess benefit for a highly compensated employee is determined as provided in the previous sentence, such excess benefit is valued again but this time at the greater of actual cost (premium payment) and the Table I rate for such employee at his actual (not 40) age with such valuation being included in his taxable income. IRC Section 89(g)(3)(C)(ii). Thus, if group term coverage over $50,000 was already included in the highly compensated employee's income at Table I rate, the discrimination sanction only affects such employees if the actual cost of excess coverage is more.

If an employer fails to report an excess benefit on a highly compensated employee's W-2, there is a penalty tax equal to the top individual marginal bracket multiplied by the excess employer provided benefit to such highly compensated employee -- greater of cost or Table I. IRC Section 6652(k).

13. <u>Insurance "Funding" Nonqualified Deferred Compensation Plans</u>

a. <u>General Concept</u>. Insurance "funding" nonqualified deferred compensation has been divided into two broad categories: salary continuation and pure deferred compensation. A pure deferred compensation plan involves an agreement between the employer and employee whereby the employee gives up some portion of present compensation, or foregoes a raise or bonus, in exchange for the employer's promise to pay a deferred benefit some time in the future. A salary continuation plan is an additional fringe benefit provided by the employer in addition to all other forms of compensation -- the employer promises to pay a deferred benefit, but there is no reduction in the employee's present compensation, raise or bonus. Since the taxation of these plans is similar, the term "deferred compensation," as used in this discussion, refers to both salary continuation and pure deferred compensation.

A nonqualified deferred compensation plan is an agreement between an employer and one or more key employees whom the employer selects. The employer promises to make future benefit payments to the key employees for services currently rendered. The benefits are typically received at the earliest of retirement, death or disability. Life insurance informally funds the plan so that the plan's costs, including benefits paid to key employees are recovered.

A deferred compensation plan benefits the employer because it helps to attract and reward high caliber individuals which strengthen the firm. If the employee leaves the business before the predetermined date, the deferred compensation plan benefits may be lost. The plan is flexible and selective. Therefore, there may be only one participant or many employees may participate in the plan. Unlike other employee benefit plans, eligibility can be based on job classification, performance or even personal preference. There is no need to tell non-participating employees about the plan. The employees benefit because they are able to enjoy additional retirement, disability and death benefits.

Life insurance creates a systematic reserve fund which produces funds to recover the costs and benefits of the plan, whenever the benefits become due.

b. Income Tax Treatment to the Employee. Generally, the employee will not incur current income tax liability, until the employee actually receives the payments. An exception to this rule occurs if the employee is in constructive receipt of the income or currently receives an economic benefit.

(1) Constructive Receipt. To avoid constructive receipt of income, the employee's rights must be subject to substantial limitations or restrictions. Reg. Sections 1.451-1 and 1.451-2. The IRS has agreed that the constructive receipt doctrine does not apply to an employee's rights in a payment (even if vested) if the agreement is entered into prior to the compensation being earned and the employer's promise to pay is not secured. Rev. Rul. 60-31, 1960-61 C.B. 174. However, the IRS will not issue a ruling on deferred compensation

unless there is either a substantial risk of forfeiture or the contract to defer is made after the beginning of the period of service for which the compensation is payable. Rev. Proc. 71-19, 1971-1 C.B. 698. The Tax Court has agreed with the IRS that constructive receipt doctrine does not apply to deferral of compensation payments when the contract of deferral was entered into prior to the services being performed. *Ray S. Robinson*, 44 T.C. 20 (1965). In a factual context that the amount of deferred compensation was not yet determinable, there are several court cases which allow parties to amend an existing deferred compensation agreement prior to the payment date but after the services had been performed. *Ernest K. Gann*, 31 T.C. 211 (1958). *Howard Viet*, 8 T.C. 809 (1947). *Commissioner v. Oates*, 207 F.2d 711 (7th Cir. 1953). *Commissioner v. Olmstead Inc. Life Agency*, 304 F.2d 16 (8th Cir. 1962). The IRS has acquiesed in the *Robinson*, *Oates*, *Viet* and *Gann* decisions.

The IRS has taken the position that existing deferred compensation contracts cannot be extended before the original payment date if the services have been performed and the amount of deferral is determinable. T.A.M. 8632003. However, in the second *Howard Viet* case, the Tax Court refused to apply constructive receipt at the original payment date of deferred compensation when the employer and employee prior to such date had agreed to a delay in such payment even though services had been performed and the amount of deferred compensation was determinable. 8 T.C.M. 919 (1949). However, the IRS distinguishes the second *Viet* case in T.A.M. 8632003 on the basis that the deferral was the result of arms length bargaining between the employer and the employee.

(2) <u>Economic Benefit</u>. To avoid an economic benefit, the employee must either rely upon the mere promise of the employer to pay benefits at a future date <u>or</u> the employer's promise is funded by property which is not transferable and is subject to a substantial risk of forfeiture. Reg. Sec. 1.83-3(e). IRC Section 83(c)(1), (2). Rev. Rul. 60-31, *supra*. If one of these

two conditions is not met, then the value of the property which the employer has set aside to fund the deferred compensation agreement will be includible in the employee's income even though the receipt of the deferred compensation or the property will occur at a future date.

In order to be subject to a substantial risk of forfeiture, the employee's rights to enjoyment of the property must be conditioned upon the future performance or the refraining from the performance of substantial services. Reg. Sec. 1.83-3(c)(1). "Substantial" is a question of fact. Reg. Sec. 1.83-3(c)(1). The regulations state that post-retirement services, such as consulting, may be substantial if the employee is expected to perform substantial services. A forfeiture by a retired employee for violating a covenant not to compete with his former employer may be a sufficient forfeiture provision based on the facts of the case, such as his or her age and likelihood of the employer to enforce the covenant. A mere promise by the employer to pay future benefits under a nonqualified deferred compensation contract is not considered property within the definition of substantial risk of forfeiture. Reg. Sec. 1.83-3(e).

(3) Funding for Internal Revenue Code Purposes. In general, deferred compensation contracts are "unfunded". The employee must rely only on the mere promise of the employer to pay the promised benefits if the employee is to avoid current taxation. Rev. Rul. 60-31, *supra*.

An unfunded plan does not prevent the employer from accumulating the required cash in the form of life insurance, mutual funds, or other investments, however, any funding must remain solely the property of the employer and always available to satisfy the employer's creditors.

The informal funding of deferred compensation plans through corporate ownership of life insurance does not result in current taxation to the insured-employee. *Casale v. Comm.*, 247 F.2d 440 (2nd Cir. 1957), acq.. Rev. Rul. 59-184, 1959-1 C.B. 65. Rev. Rul. 60-31, *supra* (ex. 2). Rev. Rul. 68-99, 1968-1 C.B. 193. Rev. Rul. 72-25, 1972-1 C.B. 127.

There is a highly criticized decision of the old Court of Claims which appears to reach a contrary result. *Goldsmith v. United States*, 586 F.2d 810 (1978). Subsequent private letter rulings ignore the *Goldsmith* result. P.L.R. 8028104. P.L.R. 8103089.

(4) Funding for ERISA Purposes. A nonqualified deferred compensation plan is an "employee pension benefit plan" under ERISA and, unless some exception applies, must meet the funding, participation, vesting, fiduciary and reporting rules of that statute. ERISA Sec. 3(2). If a deferred compensation plan had to meet the minimum vesting standards of Part 2 and the minimum funding standards of Part 3 of ERISA, then it would also be considered funded for income tax purposes under Sections 83 and 402(b) of the Internal Revenue Code. Fortunately, ERISA exempts from its vesting and funding requirements a plan which is unfunded and is maintained by an employer primarily for the purpose of providing deferred compensation for a select group of management or highly compensated employees -- so-called "top-hat" exemption. ERISA Secs. 201(2), 301(a)(3) and 401(a)(1). Neither "unfunded" nor "a select group of management or highly compensated employees" is defined by ERISA or Department of Labor regulations.

There is a DOL advisory opinion stating that a death benefit plan is not funded by insurance policies purchased by the employer on the lives of the participants if (i) the employer is named the beneficiary of the policy; (ii) the employer possesses all incidents of ownership and the policy is subject to creditors' claims, (iii) neither the plan nor the employee is given a preferred claim against the policy, (iv) there is no representation that the policy will be used to fund plan benefits or that it is being held as security for such benefits and the benefits are not limited or governed by the amount of insurance proceeds; and (v) the plan does not allow direct employee contributions to purchase the insurance. DOL Advisory Opinion 81-11A.

In a case dated prior to the release of the DOL Advisory Opinion, the employer purchase of life insurance was held to "informally fund" the plan for ERISA purposes. *Dependahl v. Falstaff Brewing Corp.*, 491 F.Supp. 1188 (E.D. Mo. 1980), aff'd. in part, 653 F.2d 1208 (8th Cir.), cert. denied, 102 S. Ct. 512, 641 (1981). The decision emphasized that the life insurance death proceeds were payable directly to the employees' beneficiaries through a settlement agreement and not to the employer and the life insurance policies were referenced in the plan documents as "funding" the plan.

There was widespread criticism expressed over the *Dependahl* decision. Then in *Belka v. Rowe Furniture Co.*, 571 F.Supp. 1249 (D. Md. 1983), the employer had purchased life insurance to "informally fund" a deferred compensation plan. Since the employer was sole beneficiary of the policies and the policies were part of the employer's general assets, the court was able to distinguish this case from *Dependahl* and held that the plan was not "funded" for ERISA purposes.

The same court which decided *Dependahl* concluded, in a later case, that a nonqualified deferred compensation plan informally funded with life insurance was not a funded plan for ERISA purposes, and thus not subject to minimum vesting and funding standards, because the employee's only right was against the employer as an unsecured creditor. *Belsky v. First National Life Insurance Company,* 818 F.2d 661 (8th Cir. 1987).

The Oklahoma Supreme Court has recently held that a plan which provided nonqualified deferred compensation benefits for a select group of management or highly compensated employees was unfunded and exempt from ERISA's participation and vesting requirements. *Loffland Brothers Company v. C.A. Overstreet*, No. 60,252 S. Ct. Oklahoma (May 17, 1988).

(5) Rabbi Trusts. Participants in a deferred compensation plan must rely on the employer's mere promise to pay benefits at a future date to avoid current income taxation. "Rabbi Trusts"

are used to give the employee some assurance, mostly psychological, that the employer has set aside sufficient assets to pay the promised benefits. The term "rabbi trust" is used to describe the use of an irrevocable trust created by an employer to hold assets which will provide future benefit payments for the participants in a deferred compensation plan. P.L.R. 8113107 approved an irrevocable trust set up by a congregation to provide deferred compensation payments to a rabbi.

In private rulings, the IRS has generally found that contributions made by an employer to an irrevocable, or "rabbi trust" to provide for the payment of nonqualified deferred compensation benefits to employees will not be taxed to the employees at the time the contributions are made. Instead, the employees will report benefits as income in the year in which the benefits are received or otherwise made available. G.C.M. 38220. P.L.R. 8113107. P.L.R. 8325100. P.L.R. 8502023. P.L.R. 8732005.

The assets placed in the trust must remain subject to the claims of the employer's general creditors. *Minor v. U.S.*, 772 F.2d 1972 (9th Cir. 1985). P.L.R. 8641039. P.L.R. 8735047.

In 1985, the DOL sent a letter to the IRS stating that the typical Rabbi Trust would not be considered funded for ERISA purposes if it was in connection with an excess benefit plan or a top-hat plan.

c. Income Tax Treatment to the Employer. The employer receives a tax deduction at the time the benefits are actually paid to the employee or beneficiary. IRC Section 404(a)(5). Rev. Rul. 60-31. 1960-1 C.B. 174. Rev. Rul. 70-435. 1970-2 C.B. 100. This applied even though the employer uses the accrual method of accounting. *Sol Jacobs, Jr.*, 45 T.C. 133 (1965). *Lundy Packing Company v. U.S.*, 302 F.Supp. 182 (E.D. N.C. 1969), aff'd. per curiam, 421 F.2d 850 (4th Cir. 1970).

The employer may purchase life insurance on the life of an employee so that funds will be available to meet its obligations under the agreement. Rev. Rul. 68-99, 1968-1 C.B. 193. The premiums paid by the employer are not income tax deductible as a business expense. IRC Section 264(a)(i). The employer receives the insurance death benefit income-tax free. IRC Section 101(a)(i).

Under current law (except for modified endowment contracts), the employer may withdraw life insurance account values up to its income tax basis or make policy loans without any income tax consequences. If the employer surrenders the life insurance policy, the surrender proceeds in excess of its income tax basis (the gain) will be taxed as ordinary income. IRC Section 72(a)(2)(B).

The employer receives no income tax deduction for amounts contributed to a Rabbi Trust, but rather deducts the benefit payments when they are included in the employee's income. Additionally, the employer is considered the owner of the trust under IRC Section 677 and therefore reports all income and is entitled to all deductions and credits generated by the trust. P.L.R. 8703061, P.L.R. 8722035.

The benefits paid by the employer to the employee must be ordinary, necessary and reasonable compensation. Rev. Rul. 60-31, *supra*. If the compensation does not meet the "reasonable" test and the employee is also a shareholder, the employee benefit will be treated as a dividend and the employer will be denied an income tax deduction. *Wilmark Services System, Inc. v. Commissioner*, F.2d 359 (2nd Cir. 1966).

Accumulated Earnings Tax and Alternative Minimum Tax. A corporation incurs an accumulated earnings tax when it retains earnings, in order to keep the shareholders from being taxed, in excess of an exempt amount equal to what is legitimately needed in the business. Earnings used to "informally" fund a deferred compensation plan have been held to serve a valid business purpose. *John P. Scripps Newspaper v. Commissioner*, 44 T.C. 453 (1965). As noted elsewhere in this paper, the corporate alternative minimum tax can be impacted by the inclusion in the book income and adjusted current earnings adjustments the increase in cash value of and the receipt of proceeds from corporate owned life insurance policies designed to "fund" deferred compensations plans.

